Guiding Those Left Behind In Illinois

LEGAL AND PRACTICAL THINGS
YOU NEED TO DO
TO SETTLE AN ESTATE IN ILLINOIS

and

HOW TO ARRANGE YOUR OWN AFFAIRS
TO AVOID UNNECESSARY COSTS
TO YOUR FAMILY

By AMELIA E. POHL, ESQ.

and Illinois Attorney
THOMAS F. McGUIRE

EAGLE PUBLISHING COMPANY OF BOCA

Copyright © 2006 by AMELIA E. POHL
All rights reserved. No part of this book may be reproduced or transmitted for any purpose, in any form and by any means, graphic, electronic or mechanical, including photocopying, recording, or by any information storage or retrieval system, without permission in writing from AMELIA E. POHL.

The purpose of this book is to provide the reader with an informative overview of the subject; but laws change frequently and are subject to different interpretations as courts rule on the meaning or effect of a law. This book is sold with the under standing that neither the authors, nor the editors, nor the publisher, nor the distributors of this book are engaging in, or rendering, legal, accounting, financial planning, or any other professional service. Pursuant to Internal Revenue Service guidance, be advised that any federal tax advice in this publication was not intended or written to be used, and it cannot be used, by any person or entity for the purpose of avoiding penalties imposed under the Internal Revenue Code (IRS Circular 230 Disclaimer). If you need legal, accounting, financial planning or any other expert advice, you should seek the services of a licensed professional.

This book is intended for use by the consumer for his or her own benefit. If you use this book to counsel someone about the law or tax matters, then that may be considered to be an unauthorized and illegal practice.

WEB SITES: Web sites appear throughout the book for the convenience of the reader only. Publication of these Web site addresses is not an endorsement by the authors, editors or publishers of this book.

EAGLE PUBLISHING COMPANY OF BOCA
4199 N. Dixie Highway, #2
Boca Raton, FL   33431   E-mail: info@eaglepublishing.com

Printed in the United States of America ISBN 1892407973
Library of Congress Catalog Card Number 200593429

Guiding Those Left Behind In Illinois

CONTENTS

CHAPTER 1: THE FIRST WEEK *1*
    AUTOPSIES *2*
    ANATOMICAL GIFTS *4*
    THE FUNERAL *10*
    THE DEATH CERTIFICATE *27*

CHAPTER 2: GIVING NOTICE OF THE DEATH *31*
    NOTIFYING SOCIAL SECURITY *32*
    NOTIFYING IRS *37*
    NOTIFYING THE BUSINESS COMMUNITY *45*

CHAPTER 3: LOCATING THE ASSETS *59*
    LOCATING RECORDS *61*
    FINDING UNCLAIMED OR ABANDONED PROPERTY . *75*
    FILING THE WILL WITH THE COURT *80*
    ACCESSING THE SAFE DEPOSIT BOX *85*

CHAPTER 4: WHAT BILLS NEED TO BE PAID? *89*
    JOINT DEBTS *92*
    NO MONEY — NO PROPERTY *95*
    PAYING THE DECEDENT'S BILLS *97*
    SOME THINGS ARE CREDITOR PROOF *104*

CHAPTER 5: WHO ARE THE BENEFICIARIES? *117*
    PROPERTY OWNED JOINTLY *118*
    PROPERTY HELD IN TRUST *127*
    THE LAWS OF DESCENT *133*
    THE RIGHTS OF A CHILD *135*
    WHEN TO CHALLENGE THE WILL *140*

CHAPTER 6: GETTING POSSESSION OF THE PROPERTY *149*
    DISTRIBUTING PERSONAL EFFECTS *150*
    TRANSFERRING THE MOTOR VEHICLE *153*
    THE SMALL ESTATE AFFIDAVIT *164*
    TRANSFERRING REAL PROPERTY *168*
    YOUR RIGHTS AS A BENEFICIARY *174*
    THE CHECK LIST *183*

CHAPTER 7: EVERYMAN'S ESTATE PLAN *187*
    AVOIDING PROBATE *188*
    GIFT TO A MINOR CHILD *193*
    THE GIFT OF REAL PROPERTY *196*
    A TRUST MAY BE THE SOLUTION (OR NOT) . . . *203*

CHAPTER 8: YOUR ILLINOIS WILL *217*
    WHY A WILL IS NECESSARY *219*
    PREPARING AND STORING YOUR WILL *226*

CHAPTER 9: YOUR ESTATE PLAN RECORD *231*
    ORGANIZING YOUR RECORDS *232*
    THE *If I Die* FILE *239*
    KEEPING UP TO DATE *242*

GLOSSARY *251*

INDEX *271*

About The Book

We tried to make this book as comprehensive as possible so there are specialized sections of the book that do not apply to the general population and may not be of interest to you. The following GUIDE POSTS appear throughout the book. You can read the section if the situation applies to you or skip the section if it doesn't. Skipping the section will not affect the continuity of the book.

GUIDE POSTS

SPOUSE — The SPOUSE POST means that the information provided is specifically for the spouse of the decedent. If the decedent was single, you can skip this section.

LAWYER — The CALL-A-LAWYER POST alerts you to a situation that may require the assistance of an attorney. See the end of this chapter for information about how to find a lawyer.

CAUTION — The CAUTION POST alerts you to a potential problem. It is followed by a suggestion about how to avoid the problem.

Special Situation — The SPECIAL SITUATION POST means that the information given in that paragraph applies to a particular event or situation; for example when the decedent dies a violent death. If the situation does not apply, you can skip the section.

v

The Organization of the Book

Guiding Those Left Behind refers to the things that need to be done in order to settle an Estate in Illinois. The purpose of this book is to guide the reader through that process. It explains:

1. How to tend to the funeral and burial
2. What agencies need to be notified
3. How to locate the decedent's property
4. What bills need (and do not need) to be paid
5. How to determine who is entitled to inherit the decedent's property
6. How to transfer the decedent's property to the proper beneficiary

We devoted a chapter to each of these six steps; and for those who are in charge of settling an Estate, we placed a CHECK LIST at the end of Chapter 6 summarizing things that need to be done. Once you read Chapters 1 through 6 you will be able to identify those problems that can happen when someone dies. Using those Chapters as a base, you can set up your own Estate Plan so that your family is not burdened by similar problems. The rest of the book (Chapters 7, 8 and 9) suggests different methods you can use to accomplish this goal.

GLOSSARY

This book is designed for the average reader. Legal terminology has been kept to a minimum. There is a glossary at the end of the book in the event you come across a legal term that is not familiar to you.

FICTITIOUS NAMES AND EVENTS

The examples in this book are based loosely on actual events; however, all names are fictitious; and the events, as portrayed, are fictitious.

Reading the Law

Where applicable, we identified the state statute or federal statute that is the basis of the discussion. We did this as a reference, and also to encourage the general public to read the law as it is written. Prior to the Internet the only way you could look up the law was to physically take yourself to the local courthouse law library or the law section of a public library. Today, all of the state and federal statutes are literally at your finger tips. They are just a mouse click away on the Internet. To look up the law all you need is the address of the Web site and the identifying number of the statute.

FEDERAL STATUTES
http://www4.law.cornell.edu/uscode
ILLINOIS STATUTES
http://www.ilga.gov/legislation

The Illinois legislature has compiled the Illinois statutes into some 67 Chapters. The chapters are numbered in multiples of 5 beginning with Chapter 5: General Provisions and continuing to Chapter 820: Employment. Each Chapter is divided into Acts, and each Act is divided into Sections. When referring to a statute we will give the number of the Chapter, Act and Section. For example, the notation (35 ILCS 200/15-25) refers to:

Chapter 35 of the Illinois Compiled Statutes
Act 200 of Chapter 35
Section 15-25 of Act 200.

To look up a statute, go to the Illinois Statute Web site, find the Chapter, and then the Act and Section within the Chapter.

If you come across a topic that you think important, you may find it both interesting and profitable to read the law as it is actually written.

Thomas F. McGuire, Esq.

THOMAS F. McGUIRE is a Partner at Arnstein & Lehr LLP. He is also a Certified Public Accountant. His practice is concentrated in the areas of estate planning, probate and trust administration, and taxation. Attorney McGuire has substantial experience representing a broad range of individuals, financial institutions and tax-exempt organizations in connection with their estate planning and administrative needs.

Attorney McGuire regularly handles complex issues involving individual and fiduciary income tax, estate, gift and generation-skipping transfer taxes. A substantial portion of his practice is also devoted to business and succession planning for family-owned and other closely held businesses.

Thomas F. McGuire is involved in handling a diverse range of matters in the Elder Law area, including guardianships; health care and property powers of attorney; living wills; revocable and irrevocable trusts; Medicaid, Medicare and Social Security issues; and the review of agreement with nursing homes, retirement homes, and "life care" facilities.

Mr. McGuire received his Bachelor of Science degree in Accountancy from the University of Illinois in 1982 and his Juris Doctorate from the University of Illinois College of Law in 1985, where he graduated as a member of the Order of the Coif (the top 10% of the class).

Thomas F. McGuire is admitted to the bar in the States of Illinois and Arizona. He is a member of the National Academy of Elder Law Attorneys, both the National and Illinois Chapters. He is a member of the Chicago Estate Planning Council, and a member of the Chicago, Illinois State and American Bar Associations.

Attorney McGuire has spoken at seminars sponsored by bar associations, financial planners, banks, and other financial institutions and agencies. These seminars covered a broad range of matters including income tax planning issues, the structuring and creation of various types of trusts and other estate planning vehicles and issues, tax issues relating to tax-exempt organizations and business and succession planning.

You can get more information about Thomas F. McGuire and his firm by visiting their Web site.
http://www.arnstein.com

Amelia E. Pohl, Esq.

Before becoming an attorney in 1985, AMELIA E. POHL taught mathematics on both the high school and college level. During her tenure as Associate Professor of Mathematics at Prince George's Community College in Maryland, she wrote several books including
Probability: A Set Theory Approach
Principals of Counting
Common Stock Sense.

During her practice of law Attorney Pohl observed that many people want to reduce the high cost of legal fees by performing or assisting with their own legal transactions. Attorney Pohl found that, with a bit of guidance, people are able to perform many legal transactions for themselves. Attorney Pohl utilizes her background as teacher, author and attorney to provide that "bit of guidance" to the general public in the form of self-help legal books that she has written. Amelia E. Pohl is currently "translating" this book for the remaining 49 states:
Guiding Those Left Behind in Maine
Guiding Those Left Behind In North Dakota
Guiding Those Left Behind In Wyoming, etc.

THE DESIGN ARTIST

LUBOSH CECH designed the cover of this book. He is a renowned artist, with extensive educational background and professional work experience. He studied design, applied art, and painting in his native Prague, Czech Republic. He also studied art in Italy at University of Bologna. Since moving to the United States in 1984, Mr. Cech has been designing art exhibitions, working as an art director, and graphic designer. Mr. Cech is a photographer and often incorporates his photographs into his art work.

Lubosh Cech is the founder of OKO DESIGN STUDIO located in Portland, Oregon. He designs promotional materials for print and digital media. He has received numerous rewards for both graphic design and painting. For more information about Mr. Cech and the OKO Design Studio visit his Web site.

http://www.okodesignstudio.com

THE PHOTOGRAPHER

The photograph that appears on the cover was taken by photographer GENE OSON.

ACKNOWLEDGMENT

When someone dies, the family attorney is often among the first to be called. Family members have questions about whether probate is necessary, who to notify, how to get possession of the assets, etc. Over the years, as we practiced in the field of Elder Law, we noticed that the questions raised were much the same family to family. We both agreed that a book answering such questions would be of service to the general public.

We also observed that those who had experience in settling the estate of a loved one were more understanding of the process, and better able to make decisions about how to arrange their own finances to avoid problems that could arise in settling an estate. We named the book **Guiding Those Left Behind**. The "Guiding" refers to the guidance that this book gives in the event that you need to settle the Estate of your loved one. It also refers to the guidance that you can give to your family by setting up your own Estate Plan so that your family is not burdened by unnecessary costs and delays in settling your estate.

We wish to thank all of the clients, whom we have had the honor and pleasure to serve, for providing us with the impetus to produce this book.

When You Need A Lawyer

The purpose of the book is to give the reader a basic understanding of Illinois law as it relates to Wills and other methods of Estate Planning. It is not intended as a substitute for legal counsel or any other kind of professional advice. If you have a legal question, you should seek the counsel of an attorney. When looking for an attorney, consider three things:
EXPERTISE, COST and PERSONALITY.

EXPERTISE

The State Bar of Illinois does not have a program to certify that an attorney is specialized in a particular area of law. This being the case, an attorney in State may not represent to the public that he/she is certified by the state as a specialist in any given area of law. Attorneys are allowed to state that they concentrate on certain areas of law or that they limit their practice to an area of law.

The Illinois State Bar Association can refer you to an attorney for the type of legal service your need. You can call them at (800) 252-8908 or if you are calling from out of state call (217) 525-1760.

You can call any of the local Bar Association for a referral within that county. The number for the Chicago Bar Association is (312) 544-2000.

The Illinois Bar Association has a Web site with the telephone number of the local Bar Associations.

ILLINOIS STATE BAR ASSOCIATION
http://www.illinoisbar.org/

One of the most reliable ways to find an attorney is through personal referral. Ask your friends, family or business acquaintances if they used an attorney for the field of law that you seek and whether they were pleased with the results. It is important to employ an attorney who is experienced in the area of law you seek. Your friend may have a wonderful Estate Planning attorney, but if you suffered an injury to your body, then you need an attorney who is experienced in Personal Injury.

COST

In addition to the attorney's experience, it is important to check what it will cost in attorney's fees. When you call for an appointment ask what the attorney will charge for the initial consultation and the approximate cost for the service you seek. Ask whether there will be additional costs such as filing fees, accounting fees, expert witness fees, etc.

If the least expensive attorney is out of your price range you can call your local county Bar Association for the telephone number of the Legal Aid office nearest you., or you can get that number from the Internet.

ILLINOIS LEGAL AID
http://www.IllinoisLegalAid.org

PERSONALITY

Of equal importance to the attorney's experience and legal fees, is your relationship with the attorney. How easy was it to reach the attorney? Did you go through layers of receptionists and legal assistants before being allowed to speak to the attorney? Did the attorney promptly return your call? If you had difficulty reaching the attorney, you can expect similar problems should you employ him.

Did the attorney treat you with respect? Did the attorney treat you paternally with a "father knows best" attitude or did he treat you as an intelligent person with the ability to understand the options available to you and the ability to make your own decision based on the information provided to you?

Are you able to understand and easily communicate with the attorney? Is he speaking to you in plain English or is his explanation of the matter so full of legalese to be almost meaningless to you?

Do you find the attorney's personality to be pleasant or grating? Sometimes people rub each other the wrong way. It is like rubbing a cat the wrong way. Stroking a cat from head to tail is pleasing to the cat, but petting it in the opposite direction, no matter how well intended, causes friction. If the lawyer makes you feel annoyed or uncomfortable, then find another attorney.

It is worth the effort to take the time to interview as many attorneys as it takes to find one with the right expertise, fee schedule and personality for you.

The First Week

Dealing with the death of a close family member or friend is difficult. Not only do you need to deal with your own emotions, but often with those of your family and friends. Sometimes their sorrow is more painful to you than what you are experiencing yourself.

In addition to the emotional impact of a death, there are many things that need to be done, from arranging the funeral and burial, to closing out the business affairs of the ***decedent*** (the person who died) and finally giving whatever property is left to the proper beneficiary.

The funeral and burial take only a few days. Wrapping up the affairs of the decedent may take considerably longer. This chapter explains what things you (the spouse or closest family member) need to do during the first week, beginning at the moment of death and continuing through the funeral.

♀ MALE GENDER USED ♂

Rather than use "he/she" or "his/her" for simplicity
(and hoping not to offend anyone)
we will refer to the decedent and his
Personal Representative using the male gender.

References to other people will be in both genders.

AUTOPSIES

In today's high tech world of medicine, doctors are fairly certain of the cause of death, but if there is a question as to the cause of death, the doctor may ask for permission to perform an autopsy. If, during his lifetime, the decedent signed a Power of Attorney for Health Care giving his Agent authority to agree to an autopsy, he can do so. If an Agent was not appointed, anyone who has the right to dispose of the body (parent, surviving spouse, child, next of kin, etc.), may give consent. An autopsy cannot be performed, if two or more people have equal rights to dispose of the body, and one objects, by telephone, or in writing, to the examining physician (410 ILCS 505/2).

The person who authorizes the autopsy must agree to pay for it because the cost of the examination is not covered under most health insurance plans. And that cost could be sizeable, running anywhere from several hundred to several thousand dollars. But it may be in the family's best interest to consent to the autopsy. The examination might reveal a genetic disorder that could be treated if it later appears in another family member. Death from a car "accident" could have been a heart attack at the wheel. Perhaps the patient who died suddenly in a hospital was misdiagnosed. The nursing home resident could have died from negligence and not old age. Even if none of these are found, knowing the cause of death with certainty is better than not knowing.

That was the case with the family of an elderly woman who was taken to the hospital complaining of stomach pains. The doctors thought she might be suffering from gallbladder disease but she died before they could effectively treat her. A doctor suggested that an autopsy be performed to determine the exact cause of death.

The woman had three daughters, one of whom objected to the autopsy: "Why spend that kind of money? It won't bring Mom back."

The daughter's wishes were respected; however over the years as they aged and became ill with their own various ailments, they would undergo physical examinations. As part of taking their medical history, doctors routinely asked "And what was the cause of your mother's death?" None could answer the question.

This is not a dramatic story. No mysterious genetic disorder ever occurred in any of her daughters, nor in any of their children. But each daughter (including the one who objected) at some point in her life was confronted with the nagging question "What did Mom die of?"

AUTOPSIES PERFORMED BY CORONER
When a person dies, the treating physician, or his authorized agent, must, within 48 hours, sign the death certificate stating the cause of death (410 ILCS 535/18). If someone dies at home from natural causes, who was under the care of a physician, the physician can sign the death certificate. The funeral director can take possession of the body. In such case, there is no need to call 911.

The police must be summoned whenever a body is discovered of a person who was not under the care of a physician, or who died suddenly either from illness, accident, suicide or foul play. The police will ask the Coroner or Medical Examiner to determine the cause of death. An autopsy will need to be performed whenever there is a suspicion that the death was not from natural causes or that the death was caused by a disease that poses a threat to the public health. The cost of the autopsy is paid for from the general fund of the county where the body is found (55 ILCS 5/3-3014).

Once the Coroner takes possession of a body, it will not be released until the examination is complete. In the interim, the family can proceed with arrangements for the funeral. The funeral director will contact the Coroner to determine when he can pick up the body and proceed with the funeral arrangements.

AUTOPSIES PERFORMED BY THE INSURANCE COMPANY

Companies that issue accident and life insurance policies often have provisions in their contract giving the company the right to perform an autopsy. The cost of the autopsy must be paid for by the insurance company, so they will not order an autopsy unless there is some important reason to do so, such as whether the cause of death is covered under that policy.

ANATOMICAL GIFTS

Hospital personnel determine whether a mortally ill patient is a candidate for an organ donation. Early on in the donor program those over 65 were not considered as suitable candidates. Today, however, the condition of the organ, and not the age, is the determining factor.

The federal government has established regional Organ Procurement Organizations throughout the United States to coordinate the donor program. There are two Organ Procurement Organizations in Illinois. **Mid-American Transplant Services** covers southern Illinois. **Gift of Hope Organ Tissue Donor Network** covers northern and central Illinois. If it is determined that the patient is a candidate, the hospital will contact the local Organ Procurement Organizations. The Organization, together with the doctor who is treating the patient, will determine whether the patient is a suitable donor.

GIFT AUTHORIZED PRIOR TO DEATH

If, before death, the decedent made an anatomical gift by signing a donor card, hospital personnel or the patient's doctor needs to be made aware of the gift in quick proximity to the time of death — preferably before death. If it is determined that the donation is medically acceptable, the gift will be made. No family member needs to give permission, provided the hospital has a copy of the decedent's unrevoked donor card (755 ILCS 50/5-5).

GIFT AUTHORIZED BY THE FAMILY

If no donor card is on record, and it is determined that the decedent is a suitable donor, someone who is specially trained will approach the family to request permission for the donation.

of Attorney for Health Care, his Agent can authorize the gift. If the decedent did not give such permission, priority to consent to the donation is determined by Illinois statute:

- 1st the decedent's Court appointed Guardian at the time of death
- 2nd surviving spouse
- 3rd an adult child
- 4th either parent
- 5th an adult brother or sister
- 6th an adult grandchild
- 7th a close friend of the decedent
- 8th the Guardian of the decedent's Estate
- 9th anyone authorized to dispose of the body

The person who is named Executor of the decedent's Will can also authorize the donation (755 ILCS 5/6-14).

Every effort must be made to contact those people with highest priority. If someone agrees to the gift and someone with higher priority objects, then no gift can be made. For example, if the sister of the decedent agrees to the gift (4th in priority) and the decedent had an adult child (2nd in priority), the child needs to be made aware of the gift.

No gift can be made if the child objects. Similarly, the statute prohibits the gift if the decedent ever refused to make a gift, or expressed an objection to someone with authority to make the gift (755 ILCS 50/5-5).

AFTER THE DONATION

Once the donation is made the body is delivered to the funeral home and prepared for burial or cremation as directed by the family. The donation does not disfigure the body so there can be an open casket viewing if the family so wishes.

Some regional Organ Procurement Organizations have an aftercare program that includes a letter of condolence to the family and an expression of gratitude for the gift. For privacy reasons, the identity of the recipient of the gift is not disclosed, but on request from the family, the local Organ Procurement Organization will give the family basic demographic information about the donation, such as the age, sex, marital status, number of children and occupation of the recipient of the gift.

GIFT FOR EDUCATION OR RESEARCH

Consider offering to release the body for the purpose of education or research in the event that the decedent signed a donor card, but was not an appropriate candidate for an organ donation.

You can offer to release the body to any of the following institutions to be used for education or research:

Anatomical Gift Association of Illinois
1540 S. Ashland Avenue, Suite 104
Chicago, IL 60608
Telephone (312) 733-5283

Southern Illinois University
School of Medicine
Department of Anatomy
Carbondale, IL 62901
Telephone (618) 536-5511

You will need to call within 24 hours of the death to determine whether the donation is acceptable. In general, they will not accept bodies from those who weigh more than 300 pounds or have died from a contagious disease or from crushing injuries.

The facility generally arranges for the transportation of the body to the school. You should ask whether there will be a transportation fee when you call to offer the donation.

The study can take up to two years to complete. At the end of the study the remains are cremated. The *cremains* (cremated remains) will be placed in a cemetery that is local to the university; or if the family wishes, the cremains will be delivered to the next of kin.

CAVEAT: Federal law prohibits payment for organ donations (42 U.S.C. 274 e). There is no ban on payments made to prepare organs or tissue for transplantation, nor is there any ban on charges made to transport bodies or body parts. Not-for-profit, as well as for-profit, companies have sprung up that are in the business of preparing and delivering body parts. These companies request donations from families — so they are not violating federal law by paying for the donation. The company prepares the body tissue or other parts of the donated body, and then distributes the parts throughout the United States to physicians, hospitals, research centers, etc. In many cases the monies charged for preparation and transportation includes a sizable profit.

If a company or organization other than your local Organ Procurement Organization approaches you to make a donation, before agreeing, you may want to learn about the company that is making the request.
> *What is the name of the company?*
> *Where are their main headquarters located?*
> *What is their primary business activity?*
> *What is the name and job description of the person making the request?*

DETERMINE THE END USE OF THE DONATION
You may want to ask what they intend to do with the tissue or body part. If it is being used for research, then what type of research? Where is the research being conducted? If it will be used for transplantation, what agency (doctor, hospital) will receive the donation and where is that agency located?

Once you have this information you can make an informed decision as to whether you wish to make the donation to that organization.

THE FUNERAL

Approximately ten percent of deaths occur suddenly because of accident, suicide, foul play or undetected illness. But, in general, death occurs after a lengthy illness, with a common scenario being that of an aged person who dies after being ill for several months, if not years. In such case, family and friends are prepared for the happening. Expected or not, the first job is the disposition of the body.

THE PREARRANGED FUNERAL

Increasingly, people are arranging, in advance, for their own funeral and burial. This makes it easier on the family both financially and emotionally. All the decisions have been made and there is no guessing what the decedent would have wanted.

If the decedent made provision for his burial, you should come across a cemetery deed or perhaps a certificate for a burial plot. If he made provision for his funeral, you should find a PRE-NEED SALES CONTRACT. If the funeral plan was paid by installments, determine whether it is paid in full. You also need to determine whether the contract was a fixed price agreement or whether there will be additional charges.

If you cannot locate the contract, but you know the decedent made provision for his burial and funeral, call the funeral home and ask them to send you a copy of the contract. If you believe the decedent purchased a funeral plan but you do not know the name of the funeral home, call the local funeral homes. Many local funeral homes are owned by national firms with computer capacity to identify people who have purchased a contract at any of their many locations.

Once you have possession of the contract, take it with you to the funeral home and go over the terms of the agreement with the funeral director. Ask whether the contract covers the entire funeral and burial, or whether there will be any additional expense.

MAKING FUNERAL ARRANGEMENTS

If the decedent died unexpectedly or without having made any prior funeral arrangements, then your first job is to choose a funeral director and make arrangements for the funeral or cremation. Most people choose the nearest or most conveniently located funeral home without comparison shopping. However, prices for these services can vary significantly from funeral home to funeral home. Savings can be had if you take the time to make a few telephone calls.

Receiving price quotes by telephone is your right under Federal law. Federal Trade Commission ("FTC") Rule 453.2 (b) (1) requires a funeral director to give an accurate telephone quote of the prices of his goods and services. Funeral homes are listed in the telephone directory under FUNERAL DIRECTORS. If you live in a small town, there may be only one or two listings. If such is the case, check out the funeral homes in the next largest city.

Funeral directors usually provide the following services:
- arrange for the transportation of the body to the funeral home and then to the burial site
- obtain burial transit permits
- arrange for the embalming or cremation of the body
- arrange funeral and memorial services and the viewing of the body
- obtain information for the death certificate
- order copies of the death certificate for the family
- have memorial cards printed.

THE FIRST WEEK

To compare prices you will need to determine:
- ❖ what is included in the price of a basic funeral plan
- ❖ whether you can expect any additional cost.

It may be necessary to have the body embalmed if you are going to have a viewing. Embalming is not necessary if you order a direct cremation or an immediate burial without a viewing. Federal Trade Commission Rule 453.5 prohibits the funeral home from charging an embalming fee unless you order the service.

If the decedent did not own a burial space, then that cost must be included when making funeral arrangements.

PURCHASING THE CASKET

When comparison-shopping, you will find that the single most expensive item in the funeral arrangement is the casket. Most funeral directors will quote you a price for a basic funeral plan that does not include the cost of the casket. Directors usually quote a range of prices for the casket, saying that you will need to come in and choose the casket at the time you contract for the funeral.

When selecting a casket you need to be aware that there may be a considerable mark-up in the price quoted by the funeral director. You do not need to go "sole source" when purchasing the casket. You can purchase the casket elsewhere and have it delivered to the funeral home to be used instead of the one offered by the funeral director. Funeral homes are required to accept caskets purchased elsewhere, and they may not charge a handling fee for accepting that casket. But if the price list given to you by the funeral home states that the price of their casket includes a specific dollar amount for basic services, then the funeral director is allowed to add that dollar amount to the charge for his services, should you purchase the casket elsewhere (FTC Rule 453.2, 453.4).

Caskets are not usually displayed for sale in a shopping mall, so most of us have no idea of the going price for a casket. With the advent of the Internet, you can learn all about the cost of any item, even a casket, by using your search engine to find a retail casket sales dealer. If you are not computer literate, you can locate the nearest retail casket sales outlet by looking in the yellow pages under **CASKETS**. You may need to look in the telephone directory for the nearest large city to find a listing. By making a call to a retail casket sales dealer, you will become knowledgeable in the price range of caskets. You can then decide what is a reasonable price for the product you seek.

The best time to do your comparison shopping is before you go to the funeral home to arrange for the funeral. Once you have determined what you should pay for the casket, it is only fair to give the funeral director the opportunity to meet that price. If you cannot reach a meeting of the minds, then you can always order the casket from the retail sales dealer and have it delivered to the funeral home.

ON-LINE FUNERAL SERVICES

The Internet is changing the way the world does business, and the funeral industry is no exception. A growing number of mortuaries are offering live Webcasts of funerals and wakes for those who are unable to pay their respects in person.

There are Web sites where you can post an obituary. There are on-line memorial chat rooms as well as on-line eulogies and testimonials. There is even a Web site that offers a posthumous e-mail service which allows people to leave final messages for friends and relatives. You can locate these services using your favorite search engine and typing in "obituaries."

THE CREMATION

Increasingly people are opting for cremation. The reasons for choosing cremation are varied, but for the majority, it is a matter of finances. The cost of cremation is approximately one-sixth that of an ordinary funeral and burial.

A major saving is the cost of the casket. No casket is necessary for the cremation and federal and state law prohibit a funeral director from requiring that you buy a casket when the body is being cremated. However, you may need to arrange for a suitable container to deliver the body to the crematory; and if you want to have a viewing of the body and/or a funeral service with the body present, you may need to purchase a disposable casket made of wood or cardboard (FTC Rule 453.3, 225 ILCS 41/15-75 (b)(12)).

If you are having a memorial service in a place of worship and no viewing of the body before the cremation, consider contracting with a facility that does cremations only.

Look in the telephone book under **CREMATION SERVICES**. You will also see cremation "societies" in the telephone book. Some are for-profit and others non-profit. You can also find advertisements for cremation services on the Internet.

ARRANGING FOR CREMATION

Illinois law sets an order of priority for those who control and who are responsible to pay for the decdent's final disposition, including cremation:

1st whoever the decedent named as his Agent to carry out written instructions for the decedent's final disposition

2nd anyone serving as Personal Representative or Executor of the decedent's Estate, who is acting according the decedent's written instructions

3rd the decedent's surviving spouse

4th his surviving adult child. If there is more than one surviving, competent, adult child, then the majority of them

5th the decedent's surviving, competent parent(s)

6th the majority of those who are next in line to inherit the decedent's Estate under the Laws of Descent

7th any public official who is in charge of the decedents's final disposition

8th if the decedent donated his body to science, or was a resident of a nursing home and signed a cremation authorization, then a representative of the institution

9th any other person or organization willing to assume legal and financial responsibility (410 ILCS 18/15).

THE OVERWEIGHT

Cremation may not be an option for those who weigh more than 300 pounds. Many cremation services do not have the facilities to handle a large body. If you weigh more than 300 pounds, you need to check with your local cremation service to determine whether this will be a problem.

THE DECEDENT WITH A PACEMAKER

Cremating a body with a pacemaker or any radiation producing device can cause damage to the cremation chamber or to the person performing the cremation. Because of the danger, Illinois statute prohibits cremation of a decedent with a pacemaker (410 ILCS 18/20, 18/35(c)). If the decedent has a pacemaker, you need to notify the cremation service and make arrangements to have the pacemaker removed prior to the cremation.

Some veterinary hospitals are implanting used pacemakers into pets who are suffering from heart disease. You might consider asking a Veterinarian to remove the pacemaker in exchange for a donation of the pacemaker to the hospital.

THE OVERWEIGHT DECEDENT

If the decedent weighs more than 300 pounds, you need to check to see if the Cremation service has facilities large enough to handle the body. If you cannot locate a crematory that can accommodate the body, you will need to make burial arrangements.

DISPOSING OF THE CREMAINS

If you contract to have the decedent cremated but neglect to pick up the cremains, then 60 days after the cremation, the crematory may dispose of the cremains and charge you for their final disposition; so it is important that you make arrangements for the final disposition of the cremains within the 60 day period (410 ILCS 18/40 (d)).

If the cremains are to be placed in a cemetery, you need to obtain a suitable urn for the burial. The container provided by the crematory can be used, or you can purchase an urn from the funeral director or crematory service director. Urns cost much less than caskets, but they can cost several hundred dollars. You may wish to do some comparison shopping by calling a retail sales casket dealer.

Many cemeteries have a separate building called a *columbarium*, which is especially designed to store urns. Some cemeteries allow the cremains of a family member to be placed in an occupied family plot or mausoleum If you wish to have the cremains placed in an occupied mausoleum or family plot, you need to call the cemetery and ask them to explain their policy as it relates to the burial of urns in occupied sites.

In Illinois, the crematory director is required to complete a *Burial Transit Permit* and forward a copy to the cemetery. If you intend to scatter the cremains at sea, or to transfer the cremains out of state, you need to get a copy of the Burial Transit Permit (410 ILCS 18/25).

SCATTERED AT SEA
The decedent may have expressed a desire to have his ashes placed at sea. The funeral director or cremation director should be able to assist you in seeing to it that these wishes are respected. Federal law prohibits the ashes from being scattered any closer than three nautical miles from land, so you will need to arrange to have a boat carry the ashes out to sea (Code of Federal Regulations, Title 40, Section 229.1).

> *Special Situation* — THE OUT OF STATE BURIAL

Many states, including Illinois, require a Burial Transit Permit for the burial or removal of the body or of the decedent's cremains from the state where the death occurred. If services are to be held in Illinois and in another state, contact a local funeral director and he will make arrangements with the out-of-state funeral home for the transportation of the body.

If you do not plan to have services conducted in Illinois, you can contact the out-of-state funeral director and ask him to effect the transfer. Many funeral homes belong to a national network of funeral homes, so both the local and the out-of-state funeral director usually have the means to make arrangements to transport the body.

TRANSPORTING CREMAINS

If the body has been cremated, you can transport the cremains yourself, either by carrying the ashes as part of your luggage or by arranging with the airline to transport the ashes as cargo. Have a certified copy of the death certificate and the Burial Transit Permit ready in the event that you need to identify the cremains of the decedent.

In these days of heightened security, it is important to call the airline before departure and ask whether they have any special regulation or procedure regarding the transportation of human ashes.

| SPOUSE | THE MILITARY BURIAL |

Subject to availability of burial spaces, an honorably discharged veteran, his unremarried spouse, and his dependent child may be buried in a national military cemetery.

Abraham Lincoln National Cemetery
Elwood, IL 60421 (815) 423-9958

Camp Butler National Cemetery
Springfield, IL 62707 (217) 492-4070

Danville National Cemetery
Danville, IL 61832 (217) 554-4550

Mound City National Cemetery
Mound City, IL 62963 (314) 260-8691

Rock Island National Cemetery
Rock Island, IL 61299-7090 (309) 782-2094

The Alton Nation Cemetery (314) 260-8691 and the Quincy National Cemetery (309) 782-2094 are closed to new interments, however, there may be space available in the grave site of a Veteran currently buried in either of these cemeteries for the cremains of a family member.

There is also a state Veterans cemetery:
Sunset Cemetery (217) 222-8641
Illinois Veterans Home
Quincy, IL 62301

An honorably discharged veteran can be buried in the national military cemetery at Arlington, Virginia. The Department of the Army is in charge of the Arlington National Cemetery. You can call the **Interment Service Branch** at (703) 607-8585 for information about having a veteran buried there.

THE FIRST WEEK *19*

> *Special Situation* — **THE COST OF A MILITARY BURIAL**

Burial space in a National Cemetery is free of charge. Cemetery employees will open and close the grave and mark it with a headstone or grave marker without cost to the family. If requested, the local Veteran's Administration ("VA") will provide the family with a memorial flag. The VA will not pay to have the body transported to the cemetery, so the family needs to make arrangements with a funeral firm to transport the remains to the cemetery.

Regardless of where an honorably discharged veteran is buried, allowances may be available for the plot, and the burial and grave marker expenses. The amount varies depending on factors such as whether the veteran died because of a service related injury. The VA will not reimburse any burial or funeral expense for the spouse of a veteran. For information about reimbursement of funeral and burial expenses you can call the VA at (800) 827-1000.

The Department of Veteran's Affairs has a Web site with information on the following topics:
- National and Military Cemeteries
- Burial, Headstones and Markers
- State Cemetery Grants Program
- Obtaining Military Records
- Locating Veterans

VA CEMETERY WEB SITE
http://www.cem.va.gov

| SPOUSE | BENEFITS FOR SPOUSE
OF DECEASED VETERAN

The surviving spouse of an honorably discharged veteran should contact the Veteran's Administration to determine whether he/she is eligible for any benefits. For example, if the decedent had minor or disabled children, his spouse may also be eligible for a monthly benefit of Dependency and Indemnity Compensation ("DIC").

Whether a surviving spouse is eligible for benefits depends on many factors including whether the decedent was serving on active duty, whether his death was service related, and the surviving spouse's assets and income. DIC benefits are discontinued should the surviving spouse remarry; however, the law allows payments to be resumed in the event that the subsequent marriage ends because of death or divorce.

For information about whether the surviving spouse is eligible for any benefit related to the decedent's military service call the VA at (800) 827-1000.

You can receive a printed statement of public policy: VA Pamphlet 051-000-00228-8 FEDERAL BENEFITS FOR VETERANS AND DEPENDENTS by sending a $7 check to:
THE SUPERINTENDENT OF DOCUMENTS
P.O. Box 371954
Pittsburgh, PA 15250-7954

Or you can download it without charge from the Internet.

VETERAN'S ADMINISTRATION
http://www.va.gov

☎ LAWYER — THE WRONGFUL DEATH

It is important to have a Personal Injury attorney investigate any accidental death, to determine whether the death was caused by the wrongful act of a person, or company. If the accident was related to the decedent's job, the family may wish to consult with a Worker's Compensation attorney as well.

The decedent's surviving spouse and next of kin (including those related through adoption) have a right to be compensated for any economic loss, including lost financial support, they suffer because of a ***wrongful death*** (a death caused by a wrongful act). The person appointed by the Court to settle the decedent's Estate is the only one who may sue for the wrongful death. He will sue for the benefit of anyone who is entitled to be compensated for the loss; and to pay for the cost of medical bills and funeral expenses either for the decedent's Estate or to reimburse another who paid these expenses.

Whatever amount is recovered for the wrongful death will be distributed by the Court to the surviving spouse and next of kin in such proportion as the Court determines to be equitable. The Court will base its decision on the percentage of dependency each person bears to the sum of the percentages of dependency of all those who were dependent on the decedent (740 ILCS 180/2).

> *Special Situation* — CRIME VICTIM COMPENSATION

The State of Illinois reimburses crime victims and/or their families, who suffer loses that are not covered by insurance, public funds or any other compensation. If the decedent died because of a criminal act, you may be eligible to be reimbursed for loses under the Illinois statute **THE CRIME VICTIMS COMPENSATION ACT (740 ILCS 45).** Compensation can be awarded for funeral and burial expenses (up to $5,000), for medical expenses, psychological counseling, lost support, lost wages, etc. Total compensation may not exceed $27,000 (740 ILCS 45/10.1).

The Office of the Illinois Attorney General administers the program. To be eligible, the following must be true:

- The decedent was an innocent victim.
- The crime was reported to authorities within 72 hours of the discovery of the body.
- There was full cooperation with law enforcement officers by the victim and/or his family.
- Application for compensation was filed within two years from the commission of the crime or discovery of the body (740 ILCS 45/6.1).

To file a claim you can call (800) 228-3368 or write to: CRIME VICTIMS COMPENSATION PROGRAM
100 West Randolph Street
Chicago, IL 60601

You can download a Crime Victims Compensation Application from the Attorney General's Web site.

THE ILLINOIS ATTORNEY GENERAL
http://www.ag.state.il.us

> **Special Situation**

THE UNCLAIMED BODY

Police make every effort to identify and locate the family of an unclaimed body. If an indigent person dies and the police know his identity, they will try to locate the family. If the identity of the decedent is unknown, or if his family is unable or unwilling to arrange for his burial, whoever is in charge of the body (jailor, sheriff, coroner, funeral director, etc.) is required to surrender the body to any medical school that requests a donation for the advancement of science (410 ILCS 510/1).

Before doing so, the person in charge of the body must give notice of the donation to the family or Guardian of the decedent. If the family wants to take responsibility for the burial, they can do so and the donation will not be made. Similarly, if the decedent left a Will stating his wishes as to the disposition of his remains, the donation cannot be made unless it was the decedent's wish to do so (755 ILCS 50/5-5).

THE INDIGENT VETERAN

As explained previously, an honorably discharged veterans can be buried without charge — with the exception of transportation costs to the veteran's cemetery. The county board or commissioner is authorized to pay expenses for the Veteran's burial, so they may be able to assist with the cost of transportation. The county will pay up to $600 to bury the indigent parent, spouse or minor child of an honorably discharged Veteran, provided the member of the family was not receiving public assistance funds at the time of his death (55 ILCS 5/5-27001, 5/5-27002, 5/5-27003).

> *Special Situation*

THE PROBLEM
FUNERAL OR BURIAL

The funeral and burial industry is well regulated by the state and federal government. Funeral directors and embalmers must be licensed with the state (225 ILCS 41/5-5). Under Illinois statute (225 ILCS 41/15-75), the following acts are subject to disciplinary action:

- Delivering goods of a lesser quality than that presented to the purchaser as a sample
- Using a false or misleading advertisement
- Paying kickbacks to generate business
- Treating anyone differently because of race, color, creed, sex, religion or national origin
- Soliciting human bodies after death or while death is imminent
- Continued practice by a person having an infectious or contagious disease
- Being convicted of a felony or misdemeanor.

Funeral directors are licensed professionals so it is unusual to have a problem with the funeral or burial or cremation. If, however, you had a bad experience with any aspect of the funeral, you can file a complaint with the state licensing agency:

Division of Professional Regulation
320 W. Washington Street
Springfield, IL 62786
Telephone (217) 785-0800

☎ LAWYER In addition to filing a complaint with the Board, you may wish to consult with an attorney who is experienced in litigation matters to learn of other legal remedies that may be available to you.

☎ LAWYER   THE MISSING BODY

Few things are more difficult to deal with than a missing person. The emotional turmoil created by the "not knowing" is often more difficult than the finality of death. The legal problems created by the disappearance are also more difficult than if the person simply died. It may take a two-part legal process — a procedure called **Administration To Collect**, to handle the missing person's affairs while he is missing, and then a final Probate proceeding if he is later found dead or declared to be dead.

In general, the Court will appoint the person named as Executor of the decedent's Will to be the Administrator to Collect. If the missing person did not have a Will, the Court will appoint the beneficiary of his Estate for the job. The Court appointed Administrator will collect the missing persons assets and use those assets to pay bills and/or support the missing person's family, all under Court supervision (755 ILCS 5/10-1, 755 ILCS 5/10-4).

If it is necessary to have an Administrator appointed to manage the decedent's affairs, you need to employ an attorney to present evidence to the Court that the person is missing and that there is a pressing need to manage the missing person's affairs. If there is no need to manage the person's affairs, Probate can begin after seven years. Courts in Illinois have ruled that a person is presumed dead if seven years have passed and he cannot be located after a diligent search (*In Re Estate of King*, 304 Ill. App.3d 479 (1999), 710 N.E.2d 1249).

THE DEATH CERTIFICATE

It is the job of the funeral director to provide information about the decedent to the local Registrar of the district where the death occurred. The Division of Vital Records will prepare a death certificate based on that information (410 ILCS 535/18).

It is important that the information you give to the funeral or cremation director is correct. You need to check the form completed by the funeral director to be sure names are correctly spelled and dates correctly written. Once the information is sent to Vital Records, it will be difficult and time consuming to make a correction.

The funeral director will order as many certified copies of the death certificate as you request. Most establishments require an original certified copy and not a photocopy so you need to order sufficient certified copies. The following is a list of institutions that may request a certified copy:

* Each insurance company that insured the decedent or his property (health insurance, life insurance, car insurance, etc.)
* Each financial institution in which the decedent had money invested (brokerage houses, banks)
* The decedent's pension fund
* Each credit card company used by the decedent
* The IRS
* The Social Security Administration
* The Vehicle Services Department
* The County Recorder in each county where the decedent owned real property.

ORDERING COPIES OF THE DEATH CERTIFICATE

Some airlines and car rental companies offer a discount for short notice, emergency trips. If you have family flying in for the funeral, you may wish to order extra copies of the death certificate so that they can obtain an airline or car rental discount.

If you wish to order certified copies of the death certificate at a later date, you can call the funeral director and ask him to do so or you can get copies from the County Clerk at the courthouse in the county of the decedent's residence.

You can obtain a certified copy of the death certificate by writing to: **Illinois Department of Public Health**
Division of Vital Records
605 W. Jefferson Street
Springfield, IL 62702-5097

The current charge is $17 for the first certified copy and $2 for each certified copy ordered at the same time. It is a good idea to first call them at (217) 782-6553 to check the cost. The Division of Vital Records will accept personal checks or money orders made payable to the Illinois Department of Public Health. The Division will forward a certified copy of the death certificate only to members of the family, or to the beneficiary of a trust or insurance policy, so you will also want to ask what information they require.

VIA THE INTERNET
You can order the death certificate from the Web site of the Vital Records section of the Illinois Department of Public Health.

VITAL RECORDS REGISTRY
http://www.idph.state.il.us/vitalrecords

About Probate

Once a person dies, all of the property he owns as of the date of his death is referred to as the **decedent's Estate.** If the decedent owned property that was in his name only (not jointly or in trust for someone) then some sort of Court procedure may be necessary to determine who is entitled to ownership of the property. The name of the Court procedure is **Probate**. We will use the term "Court" or "Probate Court" to refer to the judge who is presiding over Probate matters.

The root of the word Probate is "to prove." It refers to the first job of the Probate Court, that is, to examine proof of whether the decedent left a valid Will. The second job of the Probate Court is to appoint someone to wrap up the affairs of the decedent by paying the cost of the Probate procedure, any outstanding bills, and then distributing whatever is left to the proper beneficiary.

If the decedent left a valid Will naming someone as *Executor* of his Estate, the Court will appoint that person for the job and issue *Letters Testamentary* giving him authority to administer the Estate. If the decedent died without a Will, the Probate Court will appoint someone to be the *Administrator* of his Estate and issue *Letters of Administration.*

For simplicity we will refer to the person appointed by the Court to settle the decedent's Estate as the **Personal Representative**, and the document authorizing him to act, as his *Letters*.

There are different ways to conduct a Probate procedure depending on the value of the property that is being Probated, and whether the decedent owned real property at the time of his death. We will refer to the property that is distributed as part of a Probate proceeding as the decedent's ***Probate Estate*** and the method of conducting the Probate as the ***Estate Administration***.

Chapter 6 explains the different kinds of Estate Administration that are available in the state of Illinois.

But we are getting ahead of ourselves. First we need to determine whether a Probate procedure is necessary. To answer that question we need to know exactly what the decedent owned, so the next two chapters explain how to identify, and then locate, the decedent's assets.

Giving Notice Of The Death 2

Those closest to the decedent usually notify family members and close friends by telephone. The funeral director will arrange to have an obituary published in as many different newspapers as the family requests, but there is still the job of notifying the government and people who were doing business with the decedent. That job is the duty of whoever is appointed as Personal Representative of the decedent's Estate.

Illinois law gives an order of priority for the appointment of Personal Representative. Whoever the decedent named as Executor or Personal Representative of his Will has top priority. Once appointed, it is his job to give notice of the death.

If the decedent died without a valid Will, the surviving spouse has priority to be appointed as Personal Representative, so it is up to the spouse to let everyone know of the death (755 ILCS 5/9-3). If there is no spouse, the job falls to his next of kin. By *next of kin,* we mean those people who inherit the decedent's property according to the ILLINOIS RULES OF DESCENT AND DISTRIBUTION. Those Rules are explained in Chapter 5.

The person who has the job of settling the decedent's Estate should begin to give notice as soon as is practicable after the death. Two government agencies that need to be notified are the Social Security Administration and the IRS. This chapter gives their telephone number as well as other agencies that need to be notified.

NOTIFYING SOCIAL SECURITY

Many funeral directors will, as part of their service package, notify the Social Security Administration of the death. You may wish to check to see that this has been done. You can do so by calling (800) 772-1213. If you are hearing impaired call (800) 325-0778 TTY. You will need to give the Social Security Administration the full legal name of the decedent as well as his Social Security number and date of birth.

Special Situation — **DECEDENT RECEIVING SOCIAL SECURITY**

If the decedent was receiving checks from Social Security, you need to determine whether his last check needs to be returned to the Social Security Administration. Each Social Security check is a payment for the prior month, provided that person lives for the entire prior month. If the decedent died on the last day of the month, you should not cash the check for that month.

For example, if he died on July 31st, you need to return the check that the Social Security mailed out in August. If however, he died on August 1st the check sent in August need not be returned because that check was payment for the month of July.

If the Social Security check is electronically deposited into a bank account, notify the bank and the Social Security Administration that the account holder died. If the check needs to be returned, the Social Security Administration will withdraw it electronically from the bank account. You will need to keep the account open until the funds are withdrawn.

| SPOUSE | SPOUSE/CHILD'S SOCIAL SECURITY BENEFITS

If the decedent had sufficient work credits, the Social Security Administration will give the decedent's widow(er) or if unmarried, then the decedent's minor children, a one-time death benefit in the amount of $255.

SURVIVORS BENEFITS:

The spouse (or former spouse) of the decedent may be eligible for Survivor Benefits. Benefits vary depending on the amount of work credits earned by the decedent; whether the decedent had minor or disabled children; the spouse's age; how long they were married; etc. The minor child of the decedent may be eligible for benefits regardless of whether the child's father (the decedent) ever married the child's mother. Paternity can be established by any one of several methods including the father acknowledging his child in writing or verbally to members of his family. For more information you can call the Social Security Administration at (800) 772-1213.

SOCIAL SECURITY BENEFITS

A spouse or former spouse can collect Social Security benefits based on the decedent's work record. This value may be greater than the spouse now receives. It is important to make an appointment with your local Social Security office and determine whether you as the spouse (or former spouse) or parent of decedent's minor child are eligible for any Social Security or Survivor benefit. You can download publications that explain survivors benefits from the Social Security Web site.

SOCIAL SECURITY ADMINISTRATION
http://www.ssa.gov

> *Special Situation*

DECEDENT WITH GOVERNMENT PENSION

Any pension or annuity check received after the date of death of a federal retiree, or a survivor annuitant, needs to be returned to the U.S. Treasury. If the check is direct deposited to a bank account, call the financial institution and ask them to return the check. If the check is sent by mail, you need to return it to the return mail address on the Department of Treasury envelope in which the check was mailed. Include a letter explaining the reason for the return of the check and stating the decedent's date of death.

$$$ APPLY FOR BENEFITS $$$

A survivor annuity may be available to a surviving spouse, and/or minor or disabled child. In some cases, a former spouse may be eligible for benefits. Even though you notify the government of the death, they will not automatically give you benefits to which you may be entitled. You need to apply for those benefits by notifying the Office of Personnel Management ("OPM") of the death and requesting that they send you an application for survivor benefits. You can call them at (888) 767-6738 or you can write to:

U. S. OFFICE OF PERSONNEL MANAGEMENT
RETIREMENT OPERATIONS CENTER
Post Office Box 45
Boyers, PA 16017-4500

You will find brochures and information about Survivor's Benefits at the OPM Web site.

U.S. OFFICE OF PERSONNEL MANAGEMENT
http://www.opm.gov

> **Special Situation**

DECEDENT WITH COMPANY PENSION OR ANNUITY

In most cases, pension and annuity checks are payment for the prior month. If the decedent received his pension or annuity check before his death, then no monies need be returned. Pension checks and/or annuity checks received after the date of death may need to be returned to the company. You need to notify the company of the death to determine the status of the last check sent to the decedent.

Before notifying the company, locate the policy or pension statement that is the basis of the income. That document should tell whether there is a beneficiary of the pension or annuity funds now that the pensioner or annuitant is dead. If you cannot locate the document, use the return address on the check envelope and ask the company to send you a copy of the plan. Also request that they forward to you any claim form that may be required in order for the survivor or beneficiary to receive benefits under that pension plan or policy.

If the pension/annuity check is direct deposited to the decedent's account, ask the bank to assist you in locating the company and notifying the company of the death.

> **Special Situation**

DECEDENT WITH AN IRA or QUALIFIED RETIREMENT PLAN ("QRP")

Anyone who is a beneficiary of an Individual Retirement Account ("IRA") or a Qualified Retirement Plan ("QRP") needs to keep in mind that income taxes may not have been paid on monies placed in an IRA or QRP account. In such case, significant taxes may be due when the money is withdrawn. You need to learn what options are available to you as a beneficiary of the plan and the tax consequences of each option. You will need to ask an accountant how much will be due in taxes for each option. Once you know all the facts, you will be able to make the best choice for your circumstance.

SPOUSE

There are special options available if the spouse is the beneficiary of the decedent's IRA account. The spouse has the right to withdraw the money from the account or roll it over into the spouse's own retirement account. Although the employer can explain options that are available, the spouse still needs to understand the tax consequence of choosing any given option. It is important to consult with an accountant to determine the best way to go.

If the decedent had a QRP, the plan may permit the spouse to roll the balance of the account into a new IRA. The spouse needs to contact the decedent's employer for an explanation of the plan and all the options that are available at this time.

NOTIFYING IRS

THE FINAL INCOME TAX RETURN
The surviving spouse can file a final joint income tax return. If there is no surviving spouse, it is the Personal Representative's job to file the decedent's final return. If Probate is not necessary, whoever takes possession of the decedent's property needs to file the final federal income tax return.

Everyone who earns an income in Illinois, must also file an Illinois income tax return — even those whose primary residence is in another state. The decedent's final federal income tax return (IRS form 1040) needs to be filed by April 15th of the year following the year in which he died. The state income tax return is filed at the same time (35 ILCS 5/505). You can get information about filing the final Illinois return by calling the Illinois Department of Revenue at (800) 732-8866, or you can visit their Web site.

ILLINOIS DEPARTMENT OF REVENUE
http://www.revenue.state.il.us

You may want to keep the decedent's bank account open until you determine whether the decedent is entitled to an income tax refund. See Chapter 6 for an explanation of how to obtain a tax refund.

THE GOOD NEWS
Monies inherited from the decedent (other than IRA or QRP benefits) are generally not counted as income to you, so you do not pay federal income tax on those monies. If the monies you inherit later earn interest or income for you, then of course you will report that income as you do any other type of income.

AN ESTATE TAX FOR THE WEALTHY

Both the federal and state government have the right to impose an *Estate Tax* on property transferred to a beneficiary as a result of the death. All the property owned as of the date of death becomes the decedent's *Taxable Estate.* This includes *real property* (residential lots, condominiums etc.) and *personal property* (life insurance policies, cars, business interests, securities, IRA accounts, etc.). It includes property held in the decedent's name alone, as well as property that he held jointly or in Trust. It also includes gifts given by the decedent during his lifetime that exceeded $10,000 per person, per year. In the year 2002, the *Annual Gift Tax Exclusion* was adjusted for inflation to $11,000 (26 U.S.C 2503). For most of us, this is not a concern because no federal Estate Tax need be paid unless the decedent's Taxable Estate exceeds the federal *Estate Tax Exclusion* amount. That value is currently two million dollars and is scheduled to go even higher:

YEAR	ESTATE TAX EXCLUSION AMOUNT
2006-2008	$2,000,000
2009	$3,500,000

Under current law, the federal Estate Tax is scheduled to be phased out in the year 2010, but reinstated once again in the year 2011 with an Exclusion Amount of $1,000,000 — unless lawmakers change the tax law once again.

There is an unlimited marital tax deduction for property transferred to the surviving spouse who is a U.S. citizen; so in most cases, no Estate tax need be paid if the decedent was married. Regardless of whether taxes are due, federal and state Estate tax returns must be filed whenever the decedent's Estate exceeds the federal Estate Tax Exclusion Amount in effect as of his date of death. Both state and federal returns are due within nine months of the date of death (26 U.S.C. 6075).

THE ILLINOIS ESTATE TAX

In addition to the federal Estate Tax there is also the **ILLINOIS ESTATE AND GENERATION SKIPPING TRANSFER TAX** (35 ILCS 405). The Illinois Estate Tax used to be referred to as a "pick-up" tax, because the state collected the tax that would have gone to the federal government had it not been for the federal Estate Tax Exclusion. As explained on the previous page, the federal Exclusion for the year 2006 is two million dollars, and federal Estate Taxes are scheduled to be phased out in 2010.

In 2003, Illinois General Assembly put a cap of the amount of federal Estate Tax Exclusion that would be recognized in Illinois. For those dying after 12/31/05 and before 12/31/09, the Exclusion amount will be two million dollars. After that the Illinois Estate Tax will be based on the federal Estate Tax Exclusion that would then have been in effect under the law as it existed in 2001, namely $1,000,000 (35 ILCS 405/2).

As with the federal Estate Tax, no tax need be paid to the state of Illinois, unless the decedent's Taxable Estate exceeds the current federal Tax Exclusion. But for those Estates larger than the Exclusion value, Estate taxes will need to be paid to the federal government and the state of Illinois. And that includes property transferred within the state of Illinois regardless of whether the decedent was a resident of the state.

Both state and federal government do not tax property passing to the decedent's spouse, however, once the surviving spouse dies, all of his Estate is subject to Estate taxes. As we will see in Chapter 7, setting up a Revocable Living Trust can significantly reduce the amount of federal and STATE Estate Taxes that may need to be paid once the surviving spouse dies.

THE UN-UNIFIED GIFT TAX

Up until the year 2002, if you gave someone more than $10,000 in any given year you had to report that gift to the IRS. As explained, the federal Annual Gift Tax Exclusion is now adjusted for the cost of living and is currently $11,000. It is expected to increase to $12,000 in the year 2006. The IRS keeps a running count of amounts you give to someone that exceed the Annual Gift Tax Exclusion. Although you are required to report amounts over the Annual Exclusion value, no tax is due unless that running total is more than the federal lifetime Gift Tax Exclusion amount which is currently one million dollars. If your running total does not exceed that amount during your lifetime, once you die, the cumulative value of gifts reported to the IRS will be added to your Taxable Estate.

Up until the change in the tax law in 2001, the Gift and Estate Tax were unified. No Gift Tax needed to be paid unless the total value of the taxable gifts exceeded the federal Estate Tax Exclusion amount. That changed in 2004. In 2004, the federal Estate Tax Exclusion amount went up to $1,500,000, but the amount for the Gift Tax Exclusion remained at $1,000,000, so they are no longer unified.

To summarize:
If you make a gift to someone that is greater than the Annual Gift Tax Exclusion for that year, you must report the gift to the IRS. The IRS will keep count of values that you gave in excess of the Annual Gift Tax Exclusion. In 2004, and thereafter, if that sum exceeds $1,000,000, you will pay a Gift Tax on any amount you give that is over the Annual Gift Tax Exclusion. The Estate Tax is scheduled to be repealed in 2010, but not the Gift Tax.

Illinois does not have a Gift Tax at this time.

GIVING WITH ONE HAND — TAKING WITH THE OTHER

The current federal Estate Tax is scheduled to be phased out in the year 2010, but a new Capital Gains Tax is scheduled for 2010 that may prove even more costly than the Estate Tax. The new Capital Gains Tax is related to the way inherited property is evaluated by the federal government. Real and personal property is inherited at a "stepped-up" basis, meaning that if the decedent's property increased in value from the time he acquired it, the beneficiary inherits the property at its fair market value as of the decedent's date of death. For example, if the decedent bought stock for $20,000 and it is worth $50,000 as of his date of death, the beneficiary will take a step-up in basis of $30,000; i.e. the beneficiary inherits the stock at the current $50,000 value. If the beneficiary sells the stock for $50,000, he pays no Capital Gains Tax. If the beneficiary holds onto the stock and later sells it for $60,000, the beneficiary will pay a Capital Gains Tax only on the $10,000 increase in value since the decedent's death.

Up to 2009, there is no limit to the amount a beneficiary can take as a step-up in basis. But in 2010 caps are set in place. The decedent's Estate will be allowed a 1.3 million dollar step-up in basis, plus another 3 million for property passing to the surviving spouse (26 U.S.C. 1022(b)).

 The new law could result in significant Capital Gains Taxes that the beneficiary must pay. For example, suppose in 2010 you inherit a business from your father that he purchased for $100,000 and it is now worth 2 million dollars. There is a capital gain of 1.9 million dollars, but you are allowed a step-up in basis of only 1.3 million. If you sell it for 2 million dollars, $600,000 of your inheritance will be subject to a Capital Gains Tax.

| SPOUSE | SELLING THE HOME

In the tough "ole days" the IRS used to allow Capital Gains Tax Exclusion (up to $125,000) on the sale of one's *homestead* (the principal residence). A person had to be 55 or older to take advantage of the Exclusion, and it was a once-in-a-lifetime tax break. If a married couple sold their home and took the Tax Exclusion it was "used up" and no longer available to either partner.

In these, the good times, the IRS allows you to sell your home and up to $250,000 ($500,000 for a married couple) of the profit is free of the Capital Gains Tax. There is no limit to the number of times you can use the Exclusion, provided you own and live in the home at least two of the last five years prior to the sale (26 U.S.C. 121).

If, under the old law, the decedent and his spouse used their "once in a lifetime" Homestead Tax Exclusion, with this new law, the surviving spouse can sell the homestead and once again take advantage of a tax break.

> *Special Situation*

BENEFICIARY OF THE ILLINOIS HOMESTEAD

Illinois residents who file an Illinois income tax return are entitled to a tax credit of 5% of the real property taxes they paid on their Illinois *homestead* (i.e. primary residence) (35 ILCS 5/208). In addition, certain *Homeowners' Tax Exemptions* are allowed for real estate property tax purposes. For example a disabled veteran, or the surviving spouse of a blind person or a disabled veteran, may be eligible for a Homestead Tax Exemption. Elderly (over 65) homeowners with low income may be eligible for a "freeze" of their homestead property taxes (35 ILCS 200/15-170, 200/15-175).

If the decedent's homestead is transferred to a new owner through sale or inheritance, he must, within 30 days of the transfer, notify the Chief County Assessment Officer, in writing, of the change of ownership (35 ILCS 200/15-20). You can get the mailing address of the Chief County Assessment Officer by calling (217) 782-3627.

If the new owner is going to occupy the property as his homestead, he needs to apply for his own tax credit and/or Homestead Tax Exemption. The deadline for filing for the Senior Citizens Homestead Exemption is on or before May 31st for the year the exemption is claimed (35 ILCS 200/15-10).

You can get information about Illinois property taxes by visiting the Property Tax section of the Department of Revenue Web site.

ILLINOIS PROPERTY TAXES
http://www.ILtax.com

> *Special Situation* → **DECEDENT WITH A TRUST**

A decedent who was the **Settlor** (or *Grantor*) of a Trust, was probably managing the Trust as *Trustee* during his lifetime. The document that sets out the terms of the Trust (the *Trust Agreement)* should name a **Successor Trustee** to manage the Trust now that the Grantor is deceased. The Agreement may instruct the Successor Trustee to make certain gifts once the Settlor dies or the Trust document may direct the Successor Trustee to hold money in trust for a beneficiary of the Trust.

☎ **LAWYER** — **IF YOU ARE SUCCESSOR TRUSTEE**

If you are the Successor Trustee, in addition to following the terms of the trust, you need to obey all of the rules and provisions of the Illinois Trust and Trustees Act (760 ILCS 5). For example, you are required to give a full annual accounting (including an inventory of the trust) to all of the beneficiaries who are entitled to receive income from the Trust (760 ILCS 5/11). You should consult with an attorney experienced in Estate Planning to help you administer the Trust according to the law and without any liability to yourself.

IF YOU ARE A BENEFICIARY OF THE TRUST

If you are a beneficiary of the Trust, you need to obtain a copy of the Trust to learn how the Trust will be administered now that the Settlor is deceased. Most Trust documents are written in "legalese," so you may want to employ your own attorney to review the Trust and to explain your rights under the Trust.

NOTIFYING THE BUSINESS COMMUNITY

People and companies who were doing business with the decedent need to be notified of his death. This includes utility companies, credit card companies, banks, brokerage firms and any company that insured the decedent.

NOTIFY CREDIT CARD COMPANIES

You need to notify the decedent's credit card companies of the death. If you can find the contract with the credit card company, check to see whether the decedent had credit card insurance. If the decedent had credit card insurance, then the balance of the account is now paid in full. If you cannot find the contract, contact the company and get a copy of the contract along with a statement of the balance due as of the date of death.

DESTROY DECEDENT'S CREDIT CARDS

You need to destroy all of the decedent's credit cards. If you hold a credit card jointly with the decedent, then it is important to waste no time in closing that account and opening another in your name only.

That's something Barbara knows from hard experience. She and Hank never married but they did live together for several years before he died from liver disease. Hank came from a well to do family so he had enough money to support himself and Barbara during his long illness. Hank put Barbara on all of his credit card accounts so that she could purchase things when he became too ill to go shopping with her. After the funeral, Barbara had a gathering of friends and family at their apartment. Barbara was so preoccupied with her loss that she never noticed that Hank's credit cards were missing until the bills started coming in.

Barbara did not know who ran up the bills on Hank's credit cards during the month following his death. It was obvious that Hank's signature had been forged — but who forged it? One credit card company suspected that it might have been Barbara herself to get out of paying the bill by saying that the card had been stolen

Because the cards were held jointly, Barbara became liable to either pay the charges to the credit card or prove that she did not make the purchases. She was able to clear her credit record but it took several months and she had to employ an attorney to help her do so.

NOTIFY INSURANCE COMPANIES

Examine the decedent's financial records to determine the name and telephone number of all of the companies that insured the decedent or his property. This includes real property insurance, motor vehicle insurance, health insurance and life insurance.

MOTOR VEHICLE INSURANCE
Locate the insurance policy for any type of motor vehicle owed by the decedent (car, truck, boat, airplane) and notify the insurance company of the death. Determine how long insurance coverage continues after the death. Ask the insurance agent to explain what things are covered under the policy. Is the motor vehicle covered for all types of casualty (theft, accident, vandalism, etc.) or is coverage limited in some way?

If you can continue coverage, then determine when the next insurance payment is due. Hopefully, the car will be sold or transferred to a beneficiary before that date, but if not, you need to arrange for sufficient insurance coverage during the Probate procedure.

> **Special Situation** — ACCIDENTAL DEATH
>
> If the decedent died as a result of an accident, then check for all possible sources of accident insurance coverage, including his homeowner's policy. Some credit card companies provide accident insurance as part of their contract with their card holders. If the decedent died in an automobile accident, check to see whether he was covered by any type of travel insurance, such as rental car insurance. If he belonged to an automobile club, such as AAA, check whether accident insurance was included as part of his club membership.

LIFE INSURANCE COMPANIES

If the decedent's life was insured, you need to locate the policy and notify the company of his death. Call each life insurance company and ask what they require in order to forward the insurance proceeds to the beneficiary. Most companies will ask you to send them the original policy and a certified copy of the death certificate. Send the original policy by certified mail or any of the overnight services that require a signed receipt for the package. Make a copy of the original policy for your records before mailing the original policy to the company.

BANK ACCOUNT LIFE INSURANCE

Many banks, credit unions, and savings and loan associations provide life insurance at no cost to the primary owner of the account. While the amounts are generally small ($1,000 to $5,000), it is insurance that is often overlooked when settling the decedent's affairs. If you do not find a record of such policy, contact each financial institution to determine whether such insurance is provided by the institution.

IF YOU CANNOT LOCATE THE POLICY

If you know that the decedent was insured, but you cannot locate the insurance policy, you can contact the company and request a copy of the policy. A tougher question is how to locate the policy if you do not know the name of the insurance company. The American Council of Life Insurers offers suggestions that you may find helpful at the Missing Policy Inquiry page of its Web site.

AMERICAN COUNCIL OF LIFE INSURERS
http://www.acli.com

IF YOU CANNOT LOCATE THE COMPANY

If you cannot locate the insurance company, it may be doing business under another name or it may no longer be doing business in the state of Illinois. Each state has a branch of government that regulates insurance companies doing business in that state. If you are having difficulty locating the insurance company you can call the Department of Insurance in the state where the policy was purchased and ask for assistance in locating the company. In Illinois, you can call the Insurance Division of the Illinois Department of Financial and Professional Regulation at (217) 782-4515 or write to them at:

ILLINOIS DEPARTMENT OF
FINANCIAL AND PROFESSIONAL REGULATION
320 West Washington
Springfield, IL 62767

EAGLE PUBLISHING COMPANY OF BOCA has the telephone number of the Department of Insurance for each state at the PUBLIC INFORMATION section of its Web site.
http://www.eaglepublishing.com

WORK RELATED INSURANCE

If the decedent was employed, check his records for information about work related benefits. He may have survivor benefits from a company or group life insurance plan and/or a retirement plan. Also check with the employer about company benefits. If the decedent belonged to a union, ask the employer who you can contact to determine whether there are any union benefits.

The decedent may have belonged to a professional, fraternal or social organization such as the local Chamber of Commerce, a Veteran's organization, the Kiwanis, AARP, the Rotary Club, etc. If he belonged to any such organization, check to see whether the organization provided any type of insurance coverage.

Special Situation ▷ **BUSINESS OWNED BY DECEDENT**

If the decedent owned his own company or was a partner in a company, he may have purchased "key man" insurance. Key man insurance is a policy designed to protect the company should a valuable employee become disabled or die. Benefits are paid to the company to compensate the company for the loss of someone who is essential to the continuation of the business. Ultimately the policy benefits those who inherit the business.

If the decedent had an ownership interest in an ongoing business (sole proprietor, shareholder or partner), there may be a shareholder's or partnership agreement requiring the company to purchase the decedent's share of the business. The Personal Representative or his attorney needs to investigate to see if there was a key man insurance policy and/or such purchase agreement.

> *Special Situation*

CORPORATE OWNER OR REGISTERED AGENT

If the decedent was the sole owner and officer of a corporation, the Illinois Secretary of State, Business Services, needs to be notified of the change of ownership. There may need to be a Probate procedure to determine the new owner of the company, so it may take some period of time before new officers and directors are identified.

If the decedent was the Registered Agent of a corporation, a new agent needs to be appointed and the Secretary of State advised of the change (805 ILCS 105/5-10). Forms to change officers and statutory agents can be obtained by calling (800) 252-8980. Out of state, call (217) 782-7800.

You can download the form from the Internet.

ILLINOIS SECRETARY OF STATE
http://www.sos.state.il.us

STATUS REPORT

If you were not actively involved in running the business, you might want to call to request an abstract of the corporate record from Business Services. The report will show whether filing fees are current and will identify the officers and directors of the company. You will need to request the information in writing, so you may wish to call Business Services at (217) 782-6961 to determine what information and fee they require. Information about the company is also available at the above Web site.

HOMEOWNER'S INSURANCE

If the decedent owned his own home, check whether there is sufficient insurance coverage on the property. The decedent may have neglected to increase his insurance as the property appreciated in value. If you think the property may be vacant for some period of time, then it is important to have vandalism coverage included in the policy. Once the property is sold, or transferred to the proper beneficiary, you can have the policy discontinued or transferred to the new owner. The decedent's Estate should receive a refund for the unused portion of the premium.

MORTGAGE INSURANCE

If the decedent had a mortgage on any parcel of real estate that he owned, he might have arranged with his lender for an insurance policy that pays off the mortgage balance in the event of his death. Look at the closing statement to see whether there was a charge for mortgage insurance. Also check with the lender to determine if such a policy was purchased.

If there was no mortgage insurance, and the decedent was the sole owner, the beneficiary of the property needs to make arrangements with the lender to continue making payments on the mortgage or to refinance the loan.

NOTIFY THE HOMEOWNERS ASSOCIATION

If the decedent owned a condominium or a residence regulated by a homeowners association, the association will need to be notified of the change of ownership. Once the property is transferred, the new owner will need to contact the association to learn of the rules and regulations of the association. The new owner will need to arrange to have notices of dues and assessments forwarded to him.

HEALTH INSURANCE

The health insurance carrier probably knows of the death, but it is a good idea to contact them to determine what coverage the decedent had under that insurance plan. If you cannot find the original policy, have the insurance company send you a copy of the policy so that you can determine whether medical treatment given to the decedent before his death was covered by that policy.

> *Special Situation* ▷ **DECEDENT ON MEDICARE**
>
> If the decedent was covered by Medicare, you do not need to notify anyone, but you do need to know what things were covered by Medicare so that you can determine what medical bills are (or are not) covered by Medicare. The government publication **MEDICARE AND YOU** (Publication No. CMS-10050) explains what things are covered under Medicare and the different kinds of plans that are currently available. You can get the publication by writing to:
>
> U.S. Dept. of Health and Human Services
> Centers for Medicare and Medicaid Services
> 7500 Security Boulevard
> Baltimore, MD 21244-1850
>
> You can download the publication from the Internet.
>
> **MEDICARE WEB SITE**
> http://www.medicare.gov
>
> The publication is available on Audiotape, in Braille, in large print and in Spanish. To receive a copy you can call (800) 633-4227. TTY users call (877) 486-2048.

| SPOUSE | THE SPOUSE'S HEALTH INSURANCE

If the spouse of the decedent is insured under Medicare, then the death does not affect the surviving spouse's coverage. If the spouse was not covered by Medicare but has her own health insurance that also covered the decedent, then the spouse needs to notify the employer of the death because this may affect the cost of the plan to the employer and/or the spouse. If the spouse was covered under the decedent's policy then he/she needs to arrange for new coverage. There are state and federal laws that ensure continued coverage under the decedent's policy for a period of time depending on whether the decedent's employer falls under federal or state regulation.

If the decedent was employed by a federally regulated company (usually a company with at least twenty employees), under the Consolidated Omnibus Budget Reconciliation Act ("COBRA") the employer must make the company health plan available to the surviving spouse and any dependent child of the decedent for at least 36 months. The employer is required to give notice to the surviving spouse that the spouse and/or dependent child have the right to continue coverage under the decedent's health plan. The spouse and/or child have 60 days from the date of death or 60 days after the employer sends notice (whichever is later) to tell the employer whether the surviving spouse and child wish to continue with the health insurance plan (29 U.S.C. Sec. 1162, 1163, 1165). The only problem with continued coverage may be the cost. Before the death, the employer may have been paying some percentage of the premium. The employer has no such duty after the death unless there was some employment agreement stating otherwise.

SPOUSE'S HEALTH INSURANCE (continued)

Under COBRA, the employer may charge the spouse for the full cost of the plan plus a 2% administrative fee. If you have a question about your coverage under COBRA, you can call the U.S. Department of Labor ("DOL") at (800) 998-7542 and ask for the number of your local DOL office. You can also ask that they send you their publication **HEALTH BENEFITS UNDER COBRA**; or you can visit their Web site for more information.

> U.S. DEPARTMENT OF LABOR
> http://www.dol.gov/

HEALTH INSURANCE COVERAGE UNDER ILLINOIS LAW

For state regulated companies not covered by COBRA, the surviving spouse and/or dependent child must, within 30 days, notify the employer of the death. Within 15 days of receiving the notice, the employer must report the death to the insurance company and send a copy of the report to the spouse. The insurance company then has 30 days to offer health insurance coverage to the spouse. They must notify the spouse of the cost of the policy and include a form to accept the insurance policy. If the spouse does not accept within 30 days, the right to continue insurance benefits is terminated (215 ILCS 5/367.2, 5/367.2-5). You can get more information about continuation rights at the Division of Insurance Web site.

> ILLINOIS DIVISION OF INSURANCE
> http://www.ins.state.il.us/HealthInsurance

REFUND OF PREMIUM Under Illinois law, upon the death of a policy holder of an accident or health insurance policy, the insurance company must, upon receipt of the death certificate, refund the unearned premium pro-rated to the end of the month (215 ILCS 5/357.31).

NOTIFY ADVERTISERS

Probably the last one in the world to learn of the decedent's death is the direct mail advertiser. Advertisers are nothing if not tenacious. It is not uncommon for advertisements to be mailed to the decedent for more than ten years after the death. It is not because the advertiser is trying to sell something to the decedent, but rather the people who prepare (and sell) mailing lists do not know that he is dead.

Those who sell mailing lists may not be motivated to update the list because of the cost of doing the necessary research; and perhaps because the price of the mailing list is often based on the number of people on the list. Even those who compose their own list may decide it is less costly to mail to everyone than take the time (and money) to update the list.

If it gives you pleasure to think of advertisers spending substantial sums for nothing, then that is what you should do (nothing). But for those of you who wince each time you see another piece of mail addressed to the decedent, you can write to the Direct Marketing Association and ask that the name be deleted from all mailing lists:

Mail Preference Service
Direct Marketing Association
P.O. Box 9008
Farmingdale, NY 11735

You will need to give them the decedent's complete address, including zip code and every name variation that the decedent may have used; for example:

Theodore James Jones	T. J. Jones
Ted Jones	Ted J. Jones
T. James Jones	Jim Jones, etc.

CHANGE BENEFICIARIES

If the decedent was someone you named as beneficiary of your insurance policy, Will, Trust, brokerage account or pension plan, you may need to name another beneficiary in his place.

INSURANCE POLICY

If you named the decedent as the primary beneficiary of your life insurance policy, check to see whether you named a *contingent* (alternate) beneficiary in the event that the decedent did not survive you. If not, you need to contact the insurance company and name a new beneficiary. If you did name a contingent beneficiary, that person is now your primary beneficiary and you need to consider whether you wish to name a new contingent beneficiary at this time.

HEALTH INSURANCE POLICY

If the decedent was covered under your health insurance policy, your employer and the health insurer need to be notified of the death because this may affect the cost of the plan to you and/or your employer.

WILL OR TRUST

Most Wills provide for a contingent beneficiary in the event that the person named as beneficiary dies first. If you named the decedent as your beneficiary, check to see whether you named an alternate beneficiary. If not, you need to have your attorney revise your Will and name a new beneficiary.

Similarly, if you are the Settlor or Grantor of a Trust and the decedent was one of the beneficiaries of your Trust, check the Trust document to see if you named an alternate beneficiary. If not, contact your attorney to prepare an amendment to the Trust, naming a new beneficiary.

BANK AND SECURITIES ACCOUNTS

If the decedent was a beneficiary or joint owner of your bank or securities account, you may wish to arrange for a new beneficiary or joint owner at this time. You should make certain that your Social Security number, and not the decedent's, is used for future tax reporting purposes.

PENSION PLANS

If the decedent was a beneficiary under your pension plan, you need to notify the administrator of the plan of the death, and then name a new beneficiary. Many pension plans require that you notify them within a set period of time (usually 30 days from the date of death), so it is important to do so as soon as you are able.

If the decedent was a beneficiary of your Individual Retirement Account ("IRA") or of your Qualified Retirement Plan ("QRP") and you did not provide for an alternate beneficiary, you need to name another beneficiary. Before you choose an alternate beneficiary, it is important that you understand all of the options available to you. Not an easy task. There are many complex government regulations relating to IRA and QRP accounts. Even if you believe you understood your options when you set up your account, the federal government often changes those options.

Your choice of beneficiary might impact the amount of money you can withdraw each month, so it is important to consult with your accountant, tax attorney or financial planner, before you make your election.

NOTIFYING CREDITORS

It is the job of the person appointed as Personal Representative to notify the decedent's creditors of the death so that the creditor is given an opportunity to come forward and file a *claim* (a written demand for payment) for monies owed. The attorney for the Personal Representative usually takes care of the notice procedure. We will explain that procedure later in this book.

If no Probate proceeding is necessary, the next of kin can notify the creditors of the death, but before doing so, it is important to read Chapter 4: WHAT BILLS NEED TO BE PAID? That chapter explains what bills need to be paid and who is responsible to pay them.

Before any bill can be paid, you need to know whether the decedent left any asset that can be used to pay those debts. The next chapter explains how to identify, and then locate, all of the property owned by the decedent.

Locating the Assets 3

It is important to locate the financial records of the decedent and then carefully examine those records. Even the partner in a long-term marriage should conduct a thorough search because the surviving spouse may be unaware of all that was owned (or owed) by the decedent.

It is not unusual for a surviving spouse to be surprised when learning of the decedent's business transactions, especially in those cases where the decedent had control of family finances. One such example is that of Sam and Henrietta. They married just as soon as Sam was discharged from the army after World War II. During their marriage, Sam handled all of the finances giving Henrietta just enough money to run the household.

Every now and again Henrietta would think of getting a job. She longed to have her own source of income and some economic independence. Each time she brought up the subject Sam would loudly object. He had no patience for this new "woman's lib" thing. Sam said he got married to have a real wife — one who would cook his meals and keep house for him.

Henrietta was not the arguing type. She rationalized, saying that Sam had a delicate stomach and dust allergies. He needed her to prepare his special meals and keep an immaculate house for him. Besides, Sam had a good job with a major cruise line and he needed her to accompany him on his frequent business trips.

Once Sam retired, he was even more cautious in his spending habits. Henrietta seldom complained. She assumed the reason for his "thrift" was that they had little money and had to live on his pension.

They were married 52 years when Sam died at the age of 83. Henrietta was 81 at the time of his death. She was one very happy, very angry and very aged widow when she discovered that Sam left her with assets worth well over a million dollars!

LOCATING RECORDS

As you go through the papers of the decedent you may come across documents that indicate property ownership, such as bank registers, stock or bond certificates, insurance policies, pension or annuity records, etc. Place all evidence of ownership in a single place. You will need to contact the different companies in order to transfer title to the proper beneficiary.

To obtain the property, you may need to produce evidence of the decedent's personal relationships, such as a marriage or birth certificate, or naturalization papers, or military personnel records. If you cannot locate the decedent's marriage or birth certificate, you can get a copy of those records from the Vital Records office in the state where the event took place. Many states (including Illinois) restrict access to these records to the decedent's Personal Representative or to close family members (410 ILCS 535/25). You can use the Internet to locate vital records in the given state by using your favorite search engine to find Vital Statistics or Vital Records.

MILITARY RECORDS
The next of kin can obtain a copy of the military record of a deceased veteran by writing to:

> The National Personnel Records Center
> Military Personnel Records
> 9700 Page Avenue
> St. Louis, MO   63132-5100

They will send you form SF 180 to complete. You can fax your request to them at (301) 837-0990, or you can download the form from the Internet.

> National Archives and Records Administration
> http://www.vetrecs.archives.gov

LOCATING THE ASSETS   *61*

COLLECT AND IDENTIFY KEYS

The decedent may have kept his records in a safe deposit box, so you may find that your first job is to locate the keys to the box. As you go through the personal effects of the decedent, collect and identify all the keys that you find. If you come across an unidentified key, it could be a key to a post office box (private or federal) or a safe deposit box located in a bank or in a private vault company. You will need to determine whether that key opens a box that contains property belonging to the decedent or whether the key is to a box no longer in use. Some ways to investigate are as follows:

☑ **CHECK BUSINESS RECORDS**

If the decedent kept receipts, look through those items to see if he paid for the rental of a post office or safe deposit box. Also, look at his check register to see if he wrote a check to the Postmaster or to any safe deposit or vault company. Look at his bank statements to see if there is any bank charge for a safe deposit box. Some banks bill separately for safe deposit boxes so check with all of the banks in which the decedent had an account to determine if he had a safe deposit box with that bank.

☑ **CHECK THE KEY TYPE**

If you cannot identify the key, then take it to a local locksmith and ask whether anyone can identify the type of facility that uses such keys. If that doesn't work, go to each bank, post office and private safe deposit box company where the decedent shopped, worked or frequented and ask whether they use the type of key that you found.

☑ **CHECK THE MAIL**

Check the mail over the next several months to see if the decedent receives a statement requesting payment for the next year's rental of a post office or safe deposit box.

FORWARD THE DECEDENT'S MAIL

You may find evidence of a brokerage account, bank account, or safe deposit box by examining correspondence addressed to the decedent. If he was living alone, have his mail forwarded to the person he named as Personal Representative or Executor of his Will. If the decedent did not leave a Will, and Probate is not necessary, forward the mail to his next of kin. Call the Postmaster and ask him to send you the necessary forms to make the change. You can download the form from the U.S. Post Office Web site.

U.S. POST OFFICE
http://www.uspo.com

Request that the mail be forwarded for the longest period allowed by law (currently one year).

The decedent may have been renting a post office box at his local post office branch or perhaps at the branch closest to where he did his banking. Ask the Postmaster to help you determine whether the decedent was renting a post office box. If so, you need to locate the key to the box so that you can collect the decedent's mail.

LOST POST OFFICE BOX KEY
If the decedent had a post office box and you cannot locate the key, contact the postmaster and ask him to give you the necessary forms to complete in order to get possession of the mail in that box.

As before, have all mail addressed to that box forwarded to the Personal Representative, or if Probate is not necessary, to the decedent's next of kin.

LOCATING THE ASSETS

WHAT TO DO WITH CHECKS

You may receive checks in the mail made out to the decedent. Social Security checks, pension checks and annuity checks issued after the date of death may need to be returned to the sender. (See pages 32 and 34 of this book.) Other checks need to be deposited. If Probate is necessary, the Personal Representative will open a Probate Estate account and will deposit the decedent's checks to that account.

If no Probate procedure is necessary, then checks can be deposited to any account held in the name of the decedent. The decedent is not here to endorse the check, but you can deposit it to his account by writing his bank account number on the back of the check and printing beneath it **FOR DEPOSIT ONLY.**

The bank will accept such an endorsement and deposit the check into the decedent's account. If the check is significant in value or the decedent had different accounts that are accessible to different people, then there needs to be cooperation and a sense of fair play. If not, the dollar gain may not nearly offset the emotional turmoil.

Such was the case with Gail. Her father made her a joint owner of his checking account to assist in paying his bills. He had macular degeneration and it was increasingly difficult for him to see. The father also had a savings account that was in his name only.

Gail's brother Ken had a good paying job in Alaska. Even though he lived at a distance, Ken, his wife and two children always spent the Christmas holidays with his father and sister.

Each summer, their father enjoyed leaving the heat of Illinois to spend a few weeks in the cool Alaskan climate.

One summer, the father purchased a round trip ticket to Alaska. It cost several hundred dollars. Just before the departure date, the father had a heart attack and died. Gail called the airline to cancel the ticket. They refunded the money in a check made out to her father. She deposited the check to the joint account, and then closed it out.

As part of the Probate procedure, the money in the father's savings account was divided equally between Ken and his sister. Ken wondered what happened to the money from the airline tickets.

Gail explained "Dad paid for the tickets from the joint account, so I deposited the money back to that account. "

"Aren't you going to give me half?"

"Dad meant for me to have whatever was in that joint account. If he wanted you to have half of the money, he would have made you joint owner as well."

Ken didn't see it that way "That refund was part of Dad's Estate. It should have been deposited to his savings account to be divided equally between us. Are you going to force me to argue this in Court?"

Gail finally agreed to split the money with Ken, but the damage was done.

Gail complains that holidays are lonely since Dad died.

LOCATE FINANCIAL RECORDS

To locate the decedent's assets you need to find evidence of what he owned and where those assets are located. As you go through the papers of the decedent you should find documents that indicate property ownership, such as deeds, bank registers, title to motor vehicles, insurance policies, stock or bond certificates, etc. You will need these documents in order to transfer title to the proper beneficiary. Many people keep their financial records in a single place but it is important to check the entire house to be sure you did not miss something.

CHECK THE COMPUTER
Don't overlook that computer sitting silently in the corner. It may hold the decedent's check register and all of his financial records. You may want to monitor his E-mail for E-bank or on-line credit card accounts. The computer may be programmed to protect this information. If you cannot access the decedent's financial records, you may need to employ a computer technician or computer consultant who will be able to print out all of the information on the hard drive of the computer. You can find such a technician or consultant by looking in the telephone book under
COMPUTER SUPPORT SERVICES or
COMPUTER SYSTEM DESIGNS & CONSULTANTS.

LOCATE TITLE TO WATERCRAFT

The ILLINOIS DEPARTMENT OF NATURAL RESOURCES is in charge of the regulation of watercraft operated within the state. In Illinois, all watercraft (except sailboats) must be registered. If you cannot locate the Certificate of Number or Registration Expiration Decal, call the Department of Natural Resources for information about obtaining a duplicate (625 ILCS 45/3-1, 45/3-7. In state, call (800) 382-1696. Out of state, call (217) 557-0180.

LOCATE TITLE TO MOTOR VEHICLE

In Illinois, if monies are owed on a motor vehicle, the lender takes possession of the certificate of title until the loan is paid. If you cannot find the original certificate of title, it is either lost or monies are owed on the car and the lienholder has the title. In Illinois, the **Office of the Secretary of State** is in charge of the registration of motor vehicles. You can get information about title to the car, by writing to them at:

**Office of the Secretary of State, Record Inquiry Section
501 S. Second Street, Room 408
Springfield, IL 62756**

As of the year 2005, they charge $5 for each Title search and $5 for each Registration search. You may first want to call them at (217) 782-6992 to determine what information they require and how to obtain a duplicate title.

If you find there is a lien on the car, contact the lienholder and get a copy of the contract that is the basis of the loan.

THE LEASED CAR

You may find that the car is leased and not owned by the decedent. If so, contact the lessor and get a copy of the lease agreement. Check to see whether the decedent had life insurance as part of the agreement. If he did, then the lease may now be paid in full and the beneficiary of the car should be able to use the car for the remainder of the leasing period, or take title to the car, whichever option is available under the lease agreement. The Personal Representative (or the beneficiary) can send a certified copy of the death certificate to the leasing company with a copy of the contract and a letter requesting that the transfer be made. If the lease is not paid in full upon the decedent's death, then arrangements need to be made to satisfy the terms of the agreement. See Chapter 6 for information about transferring a leased car.

LOCATE TITLE TO MOBILE HOME

A motorized mobile homes is titled and registered in the same manner as any other motor vehicle. A ***manufactured*** or ***mobile home*** is a structure that is built on a permanent chassis (i.e. supporting frame) so constructed as to permit its transportation (430 ILCS 117/10). A manufactured/mobile home that is permanently affixed to the land is registered with the County Assessor instead of the Secretary of State (35 ILCS 515/1, 515/4). If the decedent owned a parcel of land and his mobile home was permanently attached to that land, turn to Chapter 6 for information about transferring the land and the mobile home to the proper beneficiary. If the decedent owned a mobile home that is kept in a leased space, you need to locate the lease to the mobile home lot. If you cannot locate the lease, contact the landlord for a copy, and proceed in the same manner as for a residential lease (see the next page).

LOCATE TITLE TO ALL-TERRAIN VEHICLE

As of January, 1998, All-Terrain vehicles, including off-highway motorcycles, operated within Illinois, must be titled with the Secretary of State (625 ILCS 5/3-101). If the decedent owned an All-Terrain vehicle, or an off-highway motorcycle, and you cannot locate the title to the vehicle, contact the Secretary of State at the address and telephone number as given on the previous page.

LOCATE SNOWMOBILE CERTIFICATE

All snowmobiles operated within Illinois must be registered and numbered with the Illinois Department of Natural Resources (625 ILCS 40/3-1). The snowmobile should have a Registration Expiration Decal on each side of the cowling (i.e., the metal covering of the engine). You should find a pocket size *Certificate of Number* with the same decal number. If you cannot locate the Certificate, call the Department of Natural Resources at the above number.

Special Situation — DECEDENT'S RESIDENTIAL LEASE

If the decedent was renting his residence, he may have a written lease agreement. It is important to locate the lease because the decedent's Estate may be responsible for payments under the lease. If you cannot find a lease, ask the landlord for a copy. If he reports that there was no written lease, verify that the decedent was on a month to month basis and then work out a mutually agreeable time in which to vacate the premises.

If a written lease is in effect, determine the end of the lease period, and whether the landlord is holding a security deposit. Ask whether he will agree to cancel the lease on condition that the property is promptly vacated and left in good condition. If the landlord wants to hold the Estate responsible to pay the balance of the lease, have your attorney review the lease to determine what rights and responsibilities remain now that the tenant is deceased.

☎ LAWYER — DECEDENT'S ONGOING BUSINESS

If the decedent was the sole owner of a business, or if he owned a partnership interest in a business, the Personal Representative needs to take possession of the decedent's business records and make arrangements for the operation of the business. The company accountant or company lawyer may be able to assist in obtaining the records. If you are a beneficiary of the Estate, consider consulting with your own attorney to determine what rights and responsibilities you may have in the business.

LOCATING THE ASSETS

LOCATE TITLE TO AIRCRAFT

If the decedent owned an aircraft, you should find a certificate of title to the aircraft. The Aircraft Registration Branch of the Federal Aviation Administration ("FAA") maintains aircraft records. The Aircraft Registration Branch is located in Oklahoma City, Oklahoma. Aircraft records are open to the general public, but researching the documents yourself may be difficult because the records are maintained by the registration number of the aircraft, and the Aircraft Registration Branch does not furnish lien information or the names of previous owners.

The Aircraft Registration Branch does not perform title searches, however they can give you a list of title search companies. You can call them toll free at (866) 835-5322, or visit their Web site for a list of title companies.

THE FEDERAL AVIATION ADMINISTRATION
http://www.faa.gov

In addition to locating the title, you need to find the registration for the aircraft. Illinois statute requires that all aircraft be registered with the **DIVISION OF AERONAUTICS** of the Illinois Department of Transportation (620 ILCS 5/7, 5/42). If you cannot locate the Illinois registration to the aircraft, you can call the Department of Transportation at (800) 554-0247, or you can write to them at:

Illinois Department of Transportation
Division of Aeronautics
Pilot and Aircraft Registration
1 Langhorne Bond Drive
Springfield, IL   62707-8415

COLLECT DEEDS

Collect deeds to all of the property owned by the decedent. In addition to the deed, look for other documents associated with the property, such as a mortgage. You may come across a Title Insurance policy. The new owner might be able to turn in that policy and receive a discount toward the purchase of a new title insurance, so it is important to keep the policy together with the deed.

Instead of a title insurance policy you may find an ***Abstract of Title***. An Abstract of Title is a summary of the documents or facts appearing on the public record which affect title to the property. The Abstract will need to be updated once the property is transferred. We will discuss the transfer of property in Chapter 6.

Many people keep deeds in a safe deposit box. If you cannot find the deed in the decedent's home, then you need to determine whether he had a safe deposit box and if so, you need to examine the contents of the box. See the end of this chapter for information about how to access the decedent's safe deposit box.

If you know that the decedent owned real property (lot, residential property, condominium) but you cannot find the deed, then contact the recording department in the county where the property is located. In Illinois the County Recorder is in charge of recording. He may ask you to identify the parcel of land by giving the legal description of the land or its parcel identification number. You can find this information on the last tax bill sent to the decedent. If you cannot find the last tax bill, call the County Collector or Assessor's office and they will give you the information.

LOCATING THE ASSETS   *71*

> **Special Situation** — **LOCATING THE OUT OF STATE DEED**

You need to locate the deed and any related document (Abstract of Title, title insurance policy, recorded condominium approval, etc.) to out of state property owned by the decedent.

THE LOST OUT OF STATE DEED

If you know the decedent owned out of state real property, but cannot find the deed, you can use the same procedure just described, namely, you can check with the recording department in the county where the property is located. In some states, the Clerk of the Circuit Court is in charge of the recording department. In other states it may be the Registrar of Deeds. The Clerk in the recording department should be able to give you a copy of the last recorded deed.

Many states index the property by the name of the current owner of the property, so if you know the county where the property is located, you should be able to find the deed by giving the decedent's name to the Clerk.

If you do not know the county in which the property is located, you will need to wait for the next tax bill. In many states, the tax bill contains its legal description and/or tax identification number.

COLLECT TAX RECORDS

The decedent's final federal income tax return needs to be filed. To prepare that return you may need to refer to the returns he filed for the past three years. If you cannot locate his prior tax records, check his personal telephone book and/or his personal bank register to see if he employed someone to prepare his taxes. His tax preparer should have a copy of those records.

If you are unable to locate the decedent's federal income tax returns, they can be obtained from the IRS. The IRS will send copies of the decedent's tax filings to anyone who has a *fiduciary relationship* with the decedent. The IRS considers the following people to be a fiduciary:

➢ the person appointed as the Personal Representative of the decedent's Estate
➢ the Successor Trustee of the decedent's Trust
➢ if the person died without a Will, whoever is legally entitled to possession of the decedent's property. See Chapter 5 for an explanation of the Laws of Descent.

The fiduciary can receive copies of the decedent's tax filings by notifying IRS that he/she is acting in a fiduciary capacity, and then requesting the copies. To notify the IRS of the fiduciary capacity file Form 56:
    NOTICE CONCERNING FIDUCIARY RELATIONSHIP
To request a copy of the tax return file Form 4506:
    REQUEST FOR A COPY OF TAX RETURN

Your accountant can file these forms for you or you can obtain the forms from the IRS by calling (800) 829-3676 or download them from the FORMS section of the IRS Web site.

    INTERNAL REVENUE SERVICE
    http://www.irs.gov

LOCATE STATE INCOME TAX RETURN

An Illinois income tax return must be filed if the decedent earned an income within the state of Illinois (35 ILCS 5/505). You may need last year's return to help prepare the final return. If you cannot locate it, you can obtain copies from the Illinois Department of Revenue. The procedure for obtaining a copy is much the same as that of the IRS. Even the form number is the same, namely form IL-4506.

The Department of Revenue will provide a copy of the decedent's return to anyone in a fiduciary relationship to the decedent. If the copy of the return is being requested by someone other that the decedent's spouse, the Department may require that a Personal Representative be appointed by the Court before they will forward a copy of the decedent's tax records. To get the form you can call the Illinois Department of Revenue at (217) 785-7701, or you can download it from the Internet:
http://www.revenue.state.il.us.
or write to: Records Management Division 2-202
Illinois Department of Revenue
P.O. Box 19014
Springfield, IL 62794-9014

LOCATE OUT OF STATE ACCOUNTS

If the decedent had an out of state bank or brokerage account, you might be able to locate the account through its monthly or quarterly statements. Not all financial institutions send out statements on a regular basis; however, all institutions are required to send out IRS tax form 1099 at the end of the year giving the amount of interest or dividend earned on that account. Once the forms come in, you will learn the location of the decedent's accounts that were active during the year.

FINDING UNCLAIMED OR ABANDONED PROPERTY

If the decedent was forgetful, he might have lost or abandoned property, such as a bank account, contents of a safe deposit box, a paycheck, a money order, a utility deposit, a brokerage account, travelers checks, insurance funds, etc. In general, property that is unclaimed for more than five years is presumed to be abandoned. For example, money left in a bank with no action on the account for five years, is presumed to be abandoned (765 ILCS 1025/2, 1025/2a, 1025/3, 1025/4).

Any person or institution holding abandoned property is required to turn over the property to the State Treasurer. The Treasurer will publish notice in a newspaper in the county of the last known address of the owner, saying that the property is abandoned. If a tangible item (such as jewelry) remains unclaimed, the Treasurer will convert it to cash by holding a public auction. If the owner (or his heirs) later claims the item, he will receive the net proceeds of the sale (765 ILCS 1025/12, 1025/17).

You can inquire about unclaimed property located in Illinois by calling (217) 785-6692 or by writing to:
Office of State Treasurer
Unclaimed Property Division
P.O. Box 19495
Springfield, IL 62794-9495

You can also get information about unclaimed property from the Internet.

ILLINOIS STATE TREASURER'S OFFICE
http://www.cashdash.net

THE ABANDONED WATERCRAFT

An abandoned or unclaimed watercraft will be taken into possession by a law enforcement agency, or a towing service. They will try to locate the owner by checking the records of the Department of Natural Resources. If the watercraft remains unclaimed for 30 days after notice has been sent to the owner, the law enforcement agency or the towing service will cause the ship to be sold at auction. Ten days prior to the sale, notice of the auction will be posted where the vessel was impounded (625 ILCS 45/3C-6, 45/3C-8).

Because of this relatively short period of time, it is important to determine whether the decedent owned a watercraft by calling the Department of Natural Resources at (800) 832-1696. Out of state, call (217) 557-0180.

CLAIMS IN OTHER STATES

Each state has an agency or department that is responsible for handling lost, abandoned or unclaimed property located within that state. If the decedent had residences in other states, then call the **UNCLAIMED PROPERTY** department of the state Comptroller or Treasurer to see if the decedent has unclaimed property in that state. EAGLE PUBLISHING COMPANY OF BOCA lists telephone numbers for the unclaimed property division for each state at the Public Information section of their Web site.
http://www.eaglepublishing.com

CLAIMS FOR DECEDENT VICTIMS OF HOLOCAUST

The New York State Banking Department has a special Claims Processing Office for Holocaust survivors or their heirs. The office processes claims for Swiss bank accounts that were dormant since the end of World War II. If the decedent was a victim of the Holocaust, you can get information about money that may be due to the decedent's Estate by calling (800) 695-3318.

CLAIMS FOR INCOME TAX REFUNDS

The IRS reports that each year they are unable to deliver thousands of income tax refund checks, mostly because a taxpayer moves and neglects to notify the IRS, or the U.S. Postal Service of their new address. In addition to undeliverable income tax refunds, many people are entitled to a refund but no check is sent because they fail to file an income tax return. This is often the case with employees who earned too little income to file a tax return. They may not be aware that taxes withheld from their wages are refundable. Other employees may not have had any tax withheld, but if they had a low income they might be eligible for an Earned Income Tax Credit, provided they file an income tax return. The IRS gives taxpayers three years to claim these funds. There is no penalty for filing a late return in order to qualify for these refunds.

You can determine whether the decedent is entitled to an income tax refund or a Earned Income Tax Credit by calling the IRS at (800) 829-1040. You can also get information about unclaimed tax refunds by visiting the IRS Web site.
http://www.irs.gov/

UNCLAIMED STATE INCOME TAX REFUNDS
The Illinois Department of Revenue also reports that thousands of tax refunds are returned to them each year by the U.S. Postal Service marked as "undeliverable." You can call the Department of Revenue at (800) 732-8866 to determine whether there is an unclaimed check for the decedent. Out of state call (217) 782-3336. You can also check for unclaimed income tax refund checks on the Internet.

ILLINOIS DEPARTMENT OF REVENUE
http://www.revenue.state.il.us

THE LOST PENSION

The decedent may be entitled to benefits under a pension plan of a prior employer. If the decedent worked for an employer for any significant period of time, say five years or more, check with the company benefit representative to determine whether any pension funds are owed to the decedent. If you are unable to locate the former employer, it could be that the company moved or merged with another company. There are several ways to track down the company, starting with the Illinois Secretary of State, to learn of the company's current status (see page 50).

CONTACT THE UNION
If the decedent belonged to a union, contact them and ask them to help you locate the company. They may be able to tell you whether the company is still in business, and if not, what happened to the company's pension funds.

CONTACT SOCIAL SECURITY
The Social Security Administration has the decedent's work record and the employer identification number for each of his employers. The Personal Representative can get this information by calling the Social Security Administration at (800) 772-1213.

RESEARCH THE INTERNET
Pension Benefit Guaranty Corporation insures private sector pensions. They operate an on-line search tool for those employees who did not collect their pension because the company became bankrupt or dissolved the plan, or because the company could not locate the employee. You can search their Web site by employee name or by the company name.

> PENSION BENEFIT GUARANTY CORPORATION
> http://www.pbgc.gov/search

LOCATE CONTRACTS

HEALTH CLUB CONTRACT

If the decedent belonged to a health club or gym, he may have prepaid for the year. Look for the club contract. It will give the terms of the agreement. If you cannot locate the contract, then contact the company for a copy of the agreement. If the contract was prepaid, then determine whether the agreement provides for a refund for the unused portion.

Even if the contract does not provide for a refund, you may be able to get the owner of the gym to agree to assigning the remaining membership to an heir of the decedent's Estate. Such an assignment is good public relations as well as a means of generating new business should the heir decide to purchase his own membership.

SERVICE CONTRACT

Many people purchase appliance service contracts to have their appliances serviced in the event that an appliance should need repair. If the decedent had a security system, he may have had a service contract with a company to monitor the system and contact the police in the event of a break-in.

If the decedent had a service contract, you need to locate it and determine whether it can be assigned to the new owner of the property. If the contract is assignable, the new owner can reimburse the decedent's Estate for the unused portion. If the contract cannot be assigned, then once the property is transferred, try to obtain a refund for the unused portion of the contract.

FILING THE WILL WITH THE COURT

Whoever has possession of the decedent's original Will needs to deposit it with the Probate Court in the county of the decedent's residence. If the decedent owned property in Illinois, but did not live here, the Will can be deposited with the Clerk of the Probate Court in the county where the decedent's property is located.

The judge of the Probate Court will accept an original Will only and not a copy, so it is important to hand carry the original document to the Court. If you are unable to make the delivery in person, you can mail the Will to the Clerk, but send it by registered mail so that you will have proof of delivery.

Once the Will is deposited with the Court, the Clerk keeps it until someone begins a Probate procedure. It may be that Probate is not necessary, in which case the Will remains in possession of the Court (755 ILCS 5/6-1, 5/6-7).

If you are named as Executor of the Will, you can give it to your attorney to file with the Court as part of the Probate procedure. Make a copy of the Will for your own records before delivering it to the Court or to your attorney, but do not alter the Will by removing its staples.

☎ LAWYER

PROBATING THE OUT OF STATE PROPERTY

If the decedent had his residence in Illinois and owned property in another state, you may need to conduct the initial Probate in Illinois and an *ancillary* (secondary) Probate in the other state. If the decedent had his residence in another state and owned property in Illinois, it may need to be the other way around; namely, you may need to conduct the initial Probate in the other state (755 ILCS 5/5-1).

If you are going to be Personal Representative, and the decedent was a resident of another state, before depositing the Will with the Court consult with an experienced Probate attorney <u>in each state</u> to determine where the initial Probate should be conducted. Convenience is important, but there are other things you need to consider:

COST OF PROBATE

Ask each attorney whether the location of the initial Probate procedure will have an effect on the total cost of Probate.

WHO INHERITS IF NO WILL

The Laws of Descent vary significantly state to state. If the decedent died without a Will, it is important to determine whether the location of the initial Probate procedure will change who, or how much each heir will inherit.

ESTATE/INHERITANCE TAXES

You need to determine whether the location of the initial procedure will have an impact on the amount of taxes that need to be paid.

LOCATING THE ASSETS

> *Special Situation* — **WILL DRAFTED IN ANOTHER STATE OR COUNTRY**

The state of Illinois respects the laws of other states and countries. If a Will is drafted in another state or country, the Court will allow it into Probate, provided:

- ☑ the Will was prepared and signed according to Illinois law - or -

- ☑ the Will was prepared and signed according to the laws of the state where it was drafted - or -

- ☑ the Will was prepared and signed according to the laws of the state of the decedent's residence (755 ILCS 5/7-1, 5/7-4).

See Chapter 5 for a discussion of what constitutes a valid Will in the state of Illinois.

If the Will is written in a foreign language, it will need to be accompanied by a true and complete English translation before it can be admitted to Probate.

THE MISSING WILL

People tend to put off making a Will until they think they need to. For many, that need arises when they are elderly and/or seriously ill and have property that they want to leave to someone. It is uncommon for a young person to have a Will; but those who are aged, and with significant assets, usually have one. A survey conducted for the American Association of Retired Persons ("AARP") found that the probability of having a Will increases with age. Forty-four percent of those surveyed who were between the ages of 50 to 54 had a Will. This increased to 85% for those 80 and older. You can find details of the survey at the AARP Web site.

> **AMERICAN ASSOCIATION OF RETIRED PERSONS**
> http://www.research.aarp.org

Those who make a Will usually tell the person they appoint as Executor of the existence of the Will. Chances are that someone in the decedent's circle of family and friends knows whether there is a Will. If you believe that the decedent had a Will, but you cannot find it, then there are at least three places to check out:

⇨ **THE DECEDENT'S ATTORNEY**

Look at the decedent's checkbook for the past few years and see whether he paid any attorney fees. If you are able to locate the decedent's attorney, then call and inquire whether the attorney ever drafted a Will for the decedent, and if so, whether the attorney has the original Will in his possession. If he has the Will, then ask him to forward it to the Probate Court in the county of the decedent's residence. Asking the attorney to forward the Will to the Court does not obligate you to employ the attorney should you later find that you need the assistance of an attorney for the Probate administration.

⇨ **THE CLERK OF THE PROBATE COURT**
Illinois law requires that whoever has the original Will must immediately deposit it with the Probate Court as soon as he learns of the death (755 ILCS 5/6-1). It is a good idea to check with the Clerk in the county where the decedent lived in the chance that someone found the Will and filed it with the Court.

⇨ **THE SAFE DEPOSIT BOX**
Most people keep their original Will in a safe deposit box. If you believe that the decedent had a Will but you cannot find it, check to see if the decedent had a safe deposit box. If he did, you will need to gain entry to that box to see whether the Will is in the box.

☎ LAWYER **A COPY OF THE WILL AND NO ORIGINAL**

A person can revoke his Will simply by destroying it i.e., by ripping it up, or by writing over it in such a manner as to indicate that the Will is cancelled or revoked (755 ILCS 5/4-7(a)). If you have a copy of the Will and cannot find the original, you can ask the Court to admit a copy of the Will to Probate. The Court will allow a copy of a lost Will to be probated provided it can be proven that:

☑ the document offered is a true copy of the original Will, and
☑ the decedent did not revoke his Will (755 ILCS 5/6-4).

Not easy things to prove. If you wish to have a lost Will admitted to Probate, you will need to employ an attorney experienced in Probate matters to present your case to the Court.

---

84   Guiding Those Left Behind in Illinois

ACCESSING THE SAFE DEPOSIT BOX

If the decedent was the sole lessee of a safe deposit box, upon his death access to the box will be restricted. Illinois statute 755 ILCS 15/1 allows any interested party the right to ask the bank (or safe deposit box lessor) to allow them to examine the contents of the decedent's safe deposit box. An "interested person" is anyone of the following people:

- someone who, before the decedent's death, had the right to access the box as the decedent's deputy
- the person named as Executor of the decedent's Will
- the decedent's spouse
- the decedent's parent
- the decedent's adult descendant
- the decedent's brother or sister

If none of these people are available, the bank can allow access to anyone who has a legitimate interest in having the decedent's Will filed with the Court, or who is arranging for the decedent's burial.

The bank will not allow access to the safe deposit box if the bank knows of an objection to such entry, or the box has previously been inspected according to this statute.

The interested person can examine the contents of the box provided they have the key or combination to the box and the examination is done in the presence of a bank official. If the Will is in the box, the bank will deliver it to the Clerk of the Circuit Court in the county where the decedent lived. The bank may remove any burial document found in the box and give it to the interested person.

Nothing else may be removed from the safe deposit box until someone provides proof to the bank that he is legally entitled to take possession of the remaining contents of the safe deposit box. See Chapter 6 for an explanation of what type of Probate procedure is necessary in order to get possession of the remaining items in the safe deposit box.

Before going to the bank to examine the contents of the decedent's safe deposit box, make an appointment to meet with an officer of the bank. If you are seeking access as the Executor of the Will, you need to bring a copy of the Will with you. Ask the bank what other identification they will require of you. Most banks require that you bring a certified copy of the death certificate, so you may need to wait until you receive the death certificate to prove to the bank officials that the owner of the box is dead.

Illinois statute 755 ILCS 15/1 requires that the interested person give the bank an Affidavit stating that he is an interested person and wants to examine the contents because he believes the decedent's Will is in the box. An **Affidavit** is a written statement of facts that the **Affiant** (the person signing the document) verifies as being true. You will need to sign the Affidavit in the presence of a Notary Public to verify that the statements made in the Affidavit are true.

Ask the bank if they have an Affidavit form on hand. If not you can use the form on the next page.

AFFIDAVIT PURSUANT TO ILLINOIS STATUTE 755 ILCS 15/1

BEFORE ME, this day personally appeared the Affiant, who being duly sworn, says that the following information is true and correct according to his/her best knowledge and belief:

1. My name and address are:
   _____

2. The decedent _____ (name) died on _____ A certified copy of the death certificate is attached hereto.

3. I am interested in the filing of the lessee's will or in the arrangements for his burial.

4. I believe the decedent's safe deposit box may contain his will or burial documents.

5. My relationship to the decedent is _____ and as such I am an interested person in accordance with Illinois statute.

6. No one has been appointed, or has filed a petition to be Personal Representative of the decedent's Estate.

_____
SIGNATURE OF AFFIANT

STATE OF ILLINOIS
COUNTY OF _____
Sworn to and subscribed before me on this day _____

_____
NOTARY PUBLIC

Before leaving the bank, you may want to ask an officer of the company to make an inventory of the contents of the decedent's safe deposit box using the company letterhead. You may need the inventory to present to the Court should you need an order to get possession of the contents of the box.

Once you have located the decedent's property you may think the next step is to determine who gets to inherit that property. But some of that property may be needed to pay monies owed by the decedent; so the next step is to determine what, if any, bills need to be paid.

And that is the topic of the next chapter.

What Bills Need To Be Paid? 4

The Personal Representative has the duty to be sure that all valid claims against the Estate (demands for payment) are paid. If the decedent had debts, but no money or property, then of course there is no way to pay the claim. The only remaining question is whether anyone else is responsible to pay for the monies owed. If the decedent was married, the first person the creditor will look to is the decedent's spouse. To understand the basis of this expectation, you need to know a bit of the history of our legal system.

Our laws are derived from the English Common Law. Under early English Common Law, a single woman had the right to own property in her own name and also the right to contract to buy or sell property; but when she married, her legal identity merged with her spouse. She could not hold property free from her husband's claim or control. She could no longer enter into a contract without her husband's permission.

Once married, a woman became financially dependent on her husband. He, in turn, became legally responsible to provide his wife with basic necessities — food, clothing, shelter and medical services. If anyone provided basic necessities to his wife, then regardless of whether the husband agreed to be responsible for the debt, he became obliged to pay for them. This law was called the **DOCTRINE OF NECESSARIES**.

In the early 1900's many states passed laws giving married women the right to own property and to enter into a contract without her husband's permission. Once these Married Women's Rights laws were passed, a series of Court cases tested whether the Doctrine of Necessaries still applied. Questions that judges had to decide were:

If a wife can own property and contract to pay for her own necessaries, should her husband be responsible for her debts?

And if the husband is responsible for his wife's debts, should she be responsible for his?

Some states answered "No" to both questions and passed laws repealing the Doctrine of Necessaries. Illinois answered "Well, maybe..."

The Illinois Rights of Married Persons Act states:

> Neither husband or wife shall be liable for the debts or liabilities of the other incurred before marriage, and (except as herein otherwise provided) they shall not be liable for the separate debts of each other..."

This law (750 ILCS 65/5) seems to be saying that the Doctrine of Necessaries does not apply, but the "except as herein otherwise provided" (we underlined it for emphasis) makes it quite the opposite. Somethings included in the exception are as follows:

PAYMENT AGREED TO IN WRITING
If the surviving spouse agreed, in writing, to pay for the debt of the decedent, the surviving spouse remains responsible to pay for it (750 ILCS 65/15 (a)(2)(A)).

FAMILY EXPENSE AND CHILD'S EDUCATION

Both husband and wife are responsible to pay for the expenses of the family and for the education of the children (750 ILCS 65/15 (a)(1)). "Expenses of the family" is not defined in the statute but a simple example would be the case where a husband signs a lease to rent an apartment for the family to live in. If the husband dies, then the wife is responsible to continue making payments under that lease agreement regardless of whether she signed the lease agreement.

GOODS IN POSSESSION OF THE OTHER SPOUSE

If one spouse purchases something and gives it to the other spouse, then both are equally liable to pay for the item (750 ILCS 65/15 (a)(1)(B)). For example, suppose the decedent purchased a ring for his wife and put it on his credit card. If he dies, his wife must pay the charge even though the credit card was in his name only.

But suppose the decedent used his credit card to pay for his business lunches. If his spouse did not participate in those lunches and the credit card was in his name only, then the spouse is not liable to pay that debt.

SERVICES ORDERED BY THE OTHER SPOUSE

If one spouse orders a service for the benefit of the other, then both are liable to pay for that service. This most often comes up in the context of nursing home care. Suppose the husband is ill and needs nursing care. If his wife has him admitted to a health care facility, then both are equally liable to pay for that care.

Family expenses, hospital bills, nursing home bills, legal fees, funeral expenses, must all be paid by the surviving spouse, so in essence, the Doctrine of Necessaries remains in effect in the state of Illinois.

JOINT DEBTS

A *joint debt* is a debt that two or more people are responsible to pay. Usually the contract or promissory note states that the parties agree to *joint and several liability*, meaning they all agree to pay the debt and each of them promises to be personally responsible to pay the debt.

A joint debt can also be in the form of monies owed by one person with payment guaranteed by another person. If the person who owes the money does not pay, then the *guarantor* (the person who guaranteed payment) is responsible to make payment. Funeral expenses and legal fees to Probate the decedent's Estate are all debts of his Estate. They are not joint debts unless someone guaranteed payment for monies owed.

SPOUSE — JOINT SPOUSAL DEBTS

Loans signed by the decedent and his spouse are joint debts, as are charges on credit cards that both were authorized to use. Property taxes are a joint debt if the decedent and the spouse both owned the property. All of these debts may be paid from the decedent's Estate. If there are insufficient Estate funds, the surviving spouse is liable for the entire debt.

JOINT PROPERTY BUT NO JOINT DEBT

Suppose all of the decedent's funds are held jointly with a family member and the joint owner of the bank account did not agree to pay those debts? Can the creditor require that half of the joint funds be set aside to pay the debt?

The answer to this question depends on how the account was set up. If a bank account is opened by two or more persons, each able to withdraw monies from the account, the surviving owner(s) own all of the money in the account as of the date of death. The creditor has no right to any of the account funds (765 ILCS 1005/2 (a)).

The same applies to stocks and bonds provided they were purchased so that if one owner dies, the survivor is the owner of that security. Usually the face of the security identifies the way the security was purchased. For example, if a stock or bond is issued in the name of two persons and the face of the security says they own the security as ***Joint Tenants With Right of Survivorship***; or if the security is issued to the two persons *or their survivor*, then should either of them die, the security belongs to the surviving owner. The decedent's creditors have no right to the security.

If two people own a security, it can be set up so that if one owner dies, his share goes to his heirs (and not to the surviving owner). In such case, if one owner dies, his share becomes part of his Estate and is available to pay his debts. The surviving owner still owns his own half and that is not available to the decedent's creditors.

Securities and bank accounts that are set up in this manner are identified as **Tenants-In-Common.** For example, the account or security may read:
"PETER SMITH and RAYMOND WALKER AS TENANTS IN COMMON" or "PETER SMITH and RAYMOND WALKER, T-I-C."

If the decedent held a security (or bank account) jointly with another, but no right of survivorship is stated either on the security or in the contract that established the security, the account is considered to be a Tenancy-In-Common (765 ILCS 1005/2).

NO EXEMPTION FOR TAXES
The beneficiary of the decedent's joint account has no obligation to use the joint account funds to pay the decedent's creditors; however, the decedent's share of the joint account is included as part of the decedent's Taxable Estate. If federal or state taxes are due, whoever takes the decedent's share of the joint account may be required to pay whatever taxes are due on the decedent's share of the account. But if the decedent gave instructions in his Will that all his taxes are to be paid from monies set aside for that purpose, the Personal Representative will follow those directions and pay the taxes.

NO MONEY — NO PROPERTY

If the decedent owed money, the debt needs to be paid from assets owned by the decedent — which leads to the next question "Did the decedent have any money in his own name when he died?"

If the decedent died without any money or property in his name, then there is no money to pay any creditor. The only question that remains is whether anyone else is liable to pay those bills. The issue of payment most often arises in relation to services provided by nursing homes. When a person enters a nursing home, he is usually too ill to speak for himself or even sign his name. In such cases, the nursing home administrator will ask the spouse or a family member to sign a battery of papers on behalf of the patient before allowing the patient to enter the facility. Buried in that battery of papers may be a statement that the family member agrees to be responsible for payment to the nursing home. If the family member refuses to guarantee payment and the patient's finances are limited, then the facility may refuse to admit the patient.

Under the Federal Nursing Home Reform Law, a nursing home that accepts Medicare or Medicaid payments is prohibited from requiring a family member to guarantee payment as a condition of allowing the patient to enter that facility (42 U.S.C. 13951-3(c)(5)(A)(ii)).

Nonetheless, it is common practice for a nursing home, in effect, to say "Either someone agrees to pay for the patient's bill or you need to find a different facility."

Their position is understandable. The nursing home can require payments from the patient's spouse, but if he is single, no one is responsible to make payments should the patient's monies run out. Most nursing homes are business establishments and not charitable organizations. Even not-for-profit organizations must cover their costs. The nursing home must be paid for the services they provide or they soon will be out of business. For an insolvent patient, the solution is to have the patient admitted to the facility as a Medicaid patient.

But suppose the decedent had some money when he entered the nursing home and you agreed to guarantee payment to the nursing home. What if you feel that you were coerced into signing as a guarantor?

Are you now liable to pay the decedent's final nursing home bill if your family member died without funds?

An experienced Elder Law attorney will be able to answer these questions after examining the documents that you signed and the conditions under which the patient entered the nursing home.

PAYING THE DECEDENT'S BILLS

If the decedent was married and no Probate procedure is necessary, then the surviving spouse needs to make provision for paying bills they were both responsible to pay. If the decedent was not married and he owned property belonging to him alone, such as a bank account, securities or real property, then paying monies owed by the decedent falls to the Personal Representative.

Just as soon as he is appointed, the Personal Representative is required to make a diligent effort to locate all of the decedent's creditors and notify them of the death. He will also publish notice of the death in a local newspaper. Any creditor who is not given written notice has six months from the first date that notice was published in the newspapers to come forward and present his claim (755 ILCS 5/18-3).

The Personal Representative needs to look over each claim and decide whether that claim is valid. The problem with making that decision is that the decedent is not here to say whether he actually received the goods and services that are now being billed to his Estate.

That is especially the case for medical or nursing care bills. An example of improper billing brought to the attention of this author was that of a bill submitted for a physical examination of the decedent. The bill listed the date of the examination as July 10th, but the decedent died on July 9th. Other incorrect billings may not be as obvious, so each invoice needs to be carefully examined.

If the Personal Representative decides to challenge a bill, and is unable to settle the matter with the creditor, then the Probate Court will decide whether the debt is valid and should be paid.

MEDICAL BILLS COVERED BY INSURANCE

If the decedent had health insurance you may receive an invoice stamped "THIS IS NOT A BILL." This means the health care provider has submitted the bill to the decedent's health insurance company and expects to be paid by them. If the decedent was receiving Medicare, you will receive a **Medicare Summary Notice** listing all of the services or supplies that were billed to Medicare for the prior 30 days. If the decedent was receiving Medicare Part B drugs, such as certain cancer drugs, you may receive two Medicare Summary Notices, one for the doctor's visit and for medication given to the decedent during the visit. The medication notice will let you know if the doctor administered drug is approved or denied.

Even though payment is not requested, it is important to verify that the bill is valid for two reasons:

➢ LATER LIABILITY

If the insurer refuses to pay the claim, the facility will seek payment from whoever is in possession of the decedent's property, and that may reduce the amount inherited by the beneficiaries.

➢ INCREASED HEALTH CARE COSTS

Regardless of whether the decedent was covered by a private health care insurer or Medicare, improper billing increases the cost of health insurance to all of us. Consumers pay high premiums for health coverage. We, as taxpayers, all share the cost of Medicare. If unnecessary or fraudulent billing is not checked, then ultimately, we all pay. If you believe that you have come across a case of Medicare fraud, you can call the ANTI-FRAUD HOTLINE (800) 447-8477 and report the incident to the Office of the Inspector General of the United States Department of Health and Human Services.

HOW TO CHECK MEDICARE BILLING

The structure of Medicare has changed giving people the option of staying with the *Original Medicare Plan* or choosing a *Medicare Advantage Plan* such as a Medicare Health Maintenance Organization ("HMO"), or other Medicare Health Plans. Coverage depends on which plan is chosen. You need to determine whether the decedent was covered under the Original Medicare Plan, or some other Medicare Plan. The publication *Medicare and You* explains coverage under the different options. See page 52 of this book, to obtain a copy of the booklet. Coverage under any of the other plans is explained in the membership materials given to the decedent at the time he signed up for the plan.

BILLING UNDER THE ORIGINAL MEDICARE PLAN

ASSIGNMENT

An important billing question for those under the Original Medicare Plan is whether the health care provider agreed to accept Medicare *assignment*, meaning that they agreed to accept the Medicare-approved amount. If so, the patient is responsible to pay any Medicare deductible and coinsurance amounts (usually 20% of the approved amount).

Doctors and health care providers who do not accept assignment, are limited in the amount they can charge for a Medicare covered service. The highest they can charge is **15%** over the Medicare-approved amount. This *Limiting Charge* applies only to certain services and does not apply to supplies and equipment. For more information about assignment you can call (800) 633-4227 for your free copy of *Does your doctor or supplier accept "assignment?"* or you can down-load the publication from the Medicare Web site: http://www.medicare.gov

ADVANCE BENEFICIARY NOTICE

For those who are in the Original Medicare Plan, a doctor or a supplier may give notice saying that Medicare probably will not pay for the service that is about to be provided. This is called an **Advance Beneficiary Notice**.

Other Medicare Plans also notify the patient in the event that the service is not covered under the plan. If the patient still wants the service after receiving such notice, he will be asked to sign an agreement stating that he will pay for the service in the event that Medicare does not pay.

If all of this appears confusing, it is.
To check the decedent's Medicare billing, you need the answers to the following questions:

What is the plan?
Determine whether the decedent was in the Original Medicare Plan or some other Medicare Health Plan.

What is covered under the plan?
The *Medicare and You* booklet explains what is covered under the Original Medicare Plan. You will need a copy of the membership materials for the Medicare Advantage Plans to determine what is covered under that plan.

Does the Provider accept Assignment?
If the decedent was in the Original Medicare Plan, you need to determine whether the health care provider accepted assignment; and if not, whether the Limiting Charge applies to the services provided. If assignment is accepted, or the Limiting Charge applies, you need to determine the Medicare-approved amount.

Did the decedent agree to pay?
Check to see whether the decedent was given notice that the service would not be covered by Medicare; and if so, whether he signed a contract agreeing to pay in the event that Medicare refuses to pay.

Did the decedent have Medigap Policy?
A **Medigap Policy** is a health insurance policy sold by private insurance in accordance with state and federal law. It is Medicare Supplemental Insurance. If the decedent had a Medigap Policy, get a copy of the contract and see if the goods or services provided are covered under the Policy.

DENIAL OF MEDICARE COVERAGE

If the health care provider reports to you that a service provided to the decedent is not covered by Medicare, or if the facility submits the bill and Medicare refuses to pay, check to see if you agree with that ruling by getting answers to the questions on the prior page. You can appeal that decision if you believe that the decedent was wrongly denied coverage.

If the decedent was in the Original Medicare Plan, you will find information about how to file an appeal on the Medicare Summary Notice. If he opted for a Medicare Advantage Plan or some other Medicare Health Plan, you will find that information in his health care plan materials. The book *Your Medicare Rights and Protections* (CMS Pub. No. 10112) contains information about appeals. You can get a free copy by calling (800) 633-4227 or by down-loading it from the Medicare Web site. http://www.medicare.gov.

The U.S. Department of Health and Human Services is in charge of Medicare Appeals. They hold hearings with video conference equipment or by telephone. They allow you to appeal in person before an Administrative Law Judge only if "special or extraordinary circumstances exist."

Even if an in-person hearing is allowed, Administrative Law Judges will be available in only four locations Miami, Florida; Cleveland, Ohio; Irvine, California and Arlington, Virginia. Those who insist on a face-to-face hearing lose their right to receive a decision within 90 days, so it may take considerable time before the matter is settled.

GETTING HELP WITH THE APPEAL
You can appeal the decision yourself, but it is best to first call the **Senior Health Insurance Program** ("SHIP") and learn how to present your case. You can call the Illinois Division of Insurance for the SHIP office nearest you at (800) 548-9034. Out of state call (217) 785-9021.

If you want an attorney to assist with your appeal, call the Illinois State Bar Association at (800) 252-8908. Out of state call (217) 525-1760.

Some attorneys work *pro bono* (literally for the public good; i.e. without charge) but most charge to assist in an appeal. Federal statute 42 U.S.C. 406(a)(2)(A) limits the amount an attorney may charge for a successful Medicare appeal to 25% of the amount recovered or $4,000, whichever is the smaller amount.

> **Special Situation** ▶ DECEDENT ON MEDICAID

Medicaid is a program that provides medical and long term nursing care for people with low income and limited resources. The program is funded jointly by the federal and state government. Federal law requires the state to recover monies spent from the Estate of a Medicaid recipient who was 55 or older when the decedent received Medicaid assistance. The state will seek reimbursement for the cost of nursing home care or for home based care or for other community based services (42 U.S.C. 1396p(c)).

There usually is no money to recover because to qualify for Medicaid in Illinois, a person may not have more than $2,000 in assets. But sometimes it happens that the person on Medicaid dies and his Estate later receives money perhaps as part of a settlement of a lawsuit. Also, it could happen that he owned a home in his name only. Owning a home does not disqualify a person from receiving Medicaid; however, if he received Medicaid benefits after age 55, the state has the right to place a lien on that home and seek recovery from the proceeds of the sale of the house once he dies. However, federal law prohibits any recovery of monies until the surviving spouse and/or disabled child of the decedent are deceased.

The Personal Representative needs to notify the state that they have a right to file a claim against the Estate to recover monies spent for the benefit of the decedent. He can call the decedent's caseworker for information about where to send notice.

SOME THINGS ARE CREDITOR PROOF

Sometimes it happens that the decedent had money or property titled in his name only, but he also had a significant amount of debt. In such cases the beneficiaries may wonder whether they should go through a Probate procedure if there will be little, if anything, left after the creditors are paid. Before making the decision consider that some assets are protected under Illinois law:

❖ PENSION PLANS ❖

Annuities, pensions, profit sharing or other retirement plans regulated by the federal Employee Retirement Income Security Act of 1974 ("ERISA") are creditor proof. This also includes IRA accounts, even though such accounts are not covered by ERISA (735 ILCS 5/12-1006). Monies received by a beneficiary of such plans are protected from the decedent's creditors with the following exception:

NO EXEMPTION FOR TAXES

In general, income taxes are not paid when money is placed in a retirement plan. Taxes are paid when the monies are withdrawn from the account regardless of whether the monies are withdrawn by the retiree or the person he named as beneficiary of the retirement plan. If you are inheriting money from the decedent's pension, retirement allowance, or annuity, you may need to pay taxes on those monies. You should consult with an accountant or an attorney to determine how much money needs to be set aside to pay for federal and state income taxes.

✧ LIFE INSURANCE PROCEEDS ✧

The proceeds of a life insurance, endowment or annuity policy paid to a surviving spouse, or to a child, parent, or other person who was dependent on the decedent for support, is inherited free of monies he owes (735 ILCS 5/12-1001(f)). Proceeds payable to any of these people because of the death are free of debts owed by the decedent, regardless of the value of the policy. Life insurance proceeds paid to the beneficiary are free of his debts as well, but only to the extent reasonably necessary for the support of the beneficiary (735 ILCS 5/12-1001(g)(2)).

Insurance proceeds paid to the decedent's Estate or to anyone other than the decedent's spouse, child, parent or dependent family member, are not creditor proof, and are available to pay for claims against the decedent's Estate.

✧ WRONGFUL DEATH AWARD ✧

As discussed in Chapter 1, the Personal Representative has the right to bring a lawsuit on behalf of the decedent's Estate if his death was caused by the wrongful act of a person or company. Any money awarded to the decedent's Estate because of his wrongful death goes to his surviving spouse and/or next of kin free of the decedent's debts and liabilities (740 ILCS 180/2).

Any award under the Crime Victim Compensation Act is also exempt from creditors — with the exception of products or services that were included as part of the award (740 ILCS 45/18).

❖ STATUTORY CUSTODIAL CLAIM ❖

If during the last three years of life, the decedent was disabled, and needed to be cared for by the spouse, parent, brother, sister, or child of the decedent, then the caretaker is entitled to be paid for his efforts. The Probate Court will determine the actual amount to be paid, taking into account the caretaker's lost employment opportunities, lost life-style opportunities and emotional distress suffered as a result of caring for the disabled family member. The Court will also base this ***Statutory Custodial Claim*** on the nature and extent of the disability. Subject to the amount available in the Estate, the minium amount the Court will award is: $100,000 if the decedent was 100% disabled
$75,000 if the decedent was 75% disabled
$50,000 if the decedent was 50% disabled
$25,000 if the decedent was 25% disabled
(755 ILCS 5/18-1.1).

☎ LAWYER   CLAIM MUST BE FILED

The amount awarded as a Custodial Claim comes "right off the top" of the decedent's Estate. If there are creditors or other people who will not receive anything because of a Custodial Claim, there may be a Court battle. The job of the Personal Representative's attorney is to see that the Estate is administered according to the decedent's Will — or if none, according to the Laws of Descent. If you are going to make a Custodial Claim, and you anticipate a battle, it is important to employ your own attorney to protect your interests. A Custodial Claim must be made in writing and filed with the Court in a timely manner, so you need to employ an attorney just as soon after the death as you are able.

✦ EXEMPTIONS FOR SURVIVING SPOUSE/CHILD ✦

The decedent's surviving spouse and/or minor or dependent children are entitled to take certain items of the decedent's Estate free from the claims of any of his creditors.

EXEMPT PERSONAL PROPERTY

Illinois statute exempts certain personal property from the claims of creditors, meaning that a creditor cannot take those items as payment for monies owed by the debtor. Once a debtor dies, his family (spouse and children who are living with him) are entitled to keep the decedent's Exempt Property, free of any creditor claim (735 ILCS 5/12-1003).

Exempt Personal Property includes:

➪ necessary clothing, family bible, school books, family pictures of the decedent and his dependents

➪ the decedent's interest, not to exceed $2,400, in any one motor vehicle

➪ payment because of a personal injury up to $15,000

➪ up to $1,500 of the decedent's *equity interest* (value of item less monies owed on it) in professional books or tools of the decedent's PLUS up to $4,000 in other personal property.

See Illinois statute (735 ILCS 5/12-1001) for a complete list of Exempt Personal Property.

THE SPOUSE'S AWARD

The decedent's spouse is entitled to support for nine months following the death. The amount is determined by the Probate Court after considering the life style enjoyed by the couple prior to death and how much money there is in the Estate. The minimum spousal award is $10,000 plus $5,000 for each minor or dependent child living with the surviving spouse. This money is exempt from any claim made by a creditor of the decedent. In fact, if the spouse dies before the award is paid in full, the balance of the spouse's award goes to the spouse's Estate (755 ILCS 5/15-1).

☎ LAWYER — **WILL PROVIDES FOR SUPPORT OF SPOUSE**

If the decedent's Will says in effect "The money I give to my spouse in this Will is intended to be in lieu of (in place of) the Spouse's Award," then that gift can replace the Spouse's Award (755 ILCS 5/15-1(b)). But there is a potential problem associated with accepting the gift. If the decedent had many debts, those debts must be paid before any gift can be made. If the spouse agrees to accept the gift in place of the Spouse's Award, it could be that the spouse comes away with nothing after all the debts are paid. In such case, it is better to renounce the gift and ask the Court to award money to support the spouse for nine months.

The job of the Personal Representative is to settle the decedent's Estate impartially, and without favor to any one person. If the spouse is not the Personal Representative, and there are considerable debts, the spouse should consider employing an attorney to represent his/her interests and that of the decedent's dependent children, if any.

THE CHILD'S AWARD

If the decedent had a minor or adult dependent child, that child is entitled to support for nine months following the death. An adult dependent child is someone who is unable to support himself and who is likely to become a public charge. The amount of the child's award depends on the child's life-style prior to the death, with $5,000 as the least amount of money that the Court can award. The child is entitled to the award, regardless of whether the child resides with the surviving spouse.

If there is no surviving spouse, the minimum award to the minor and adult dependent children is $10,000 plus $5,000 per child. As with the spouse's award, the child's award is creditor proof (755 ILCS 5/15-1, 5/15-2).

THE HOMESTEAD EXEMPTION

Every resident of the state of Illinois is entitled to a *Homestead Exemption* of $15,0000. If the principal residence is owned jointly, up to $30,000 is creditor proof. This does not mean the creditor cannot force the sale of the property. It just means that if the property is sold to pay the homeowner's debts, the first $15,000 ($30,000 if owned jointly) of the proceeds of the sale goes to the owner.

If the decedent owned his home in his name only, the Homestead Exemption continues for the benefit of his surviving spouse for as long as she continues to occupy the home. If the decedent had a minor child, the Homestead Exemption continues for the benefit of his minor child until he reaches 18. If the decedent is not survived by spouse or minor child, all of the value of the homestead is available to pay creditor claims (735 ILCS 5/12-901, 5/12-902).

✧ THERE IS A PRIORITY OF PAYMENT ✧

Next, consider that not all Probate debts are equal. If there are insufficient funds in the Probate Estate to pay for all claims against the decedent's Estate, then Illinois Statute (755 ILCS 5/18-10) establishes an order of priority for payment:

CLASS 1: FUNERAL, PROBATE EXPENSES and CUSTODIAL CLAIMS

FUNERAL EXPENSES

Anyone (including the spouse) who paid for the reasonable funeral and burial expenses of the decedent is entitled to be reimbursed. Burial expenses include a marker for the burial space and care of the burial site. If these monies are not promptly paid, the person who paid for these items is entitled to interest, beginning 60 days from the day the monies were due, at a rate of up to 9% per annum as allowed by contract or law.

EXPENSES OF ADMINISTRATION

If Probate is necessary, all of the fees and costs must be paid. This includes filing fees, the cost of publishing notices, reasonable attorney and Personal Representative fees.

CUSTODIAL CLAIMS

As explained on page 106, if the decedent was disabled during the last three years of his life, his family caretaker is entitled to be paid for that care. The monies paid are free of any creditor's claim.

CLASS 2: THE SURVIVING SPOUSE/CHILD AWARD

As explained on the prior page, if the decedent was married, or had minor or dependent children, they are entitled to receive support payments for the nine months following his death. The spouse or Guardian of the child needs to have the Personal Representative apply for the award as soon as the Probate proceedings begins.

CLASS 3: MONIES DUE TO THE UNITED STATES
If the decedent owed back taxes to the IRS, or if the decedent had a school loan backed by the federal government, these debts are third in priority of payment.

CLASS 4: EXPENSES OF LAST ILLNESS AND PAYROLL DEBTS
The expenses of the decedent's last illness are fourth in line for payment.

If the decedent employed workers, and owed them money for work done within the four months of his death, they are included as a Class 4 debt. Each employee is limited to a maximum of $800 as payment in this class. If more than $800 is due, then the employee can file a claim for the balance of the payment as a Class 7 debtor.

CLASS 5: MONIES HELD IN TRUST BY THE DECEDENT
If the decedent was holding money (or property) in trust for someone or for some business enterprise, and the Trust property cannot be found, the beneficiaries of the Trust can make a claim on the decedent's estate for the missing property. Such claims are a Class 5 debt.

CLASS 6: MONIES OWED TO THE STATE
As explained on page 103, the state is entitled to be reimbursed for medical assistance given to the decedent after age 55. Medicaid claims are 6th in priority, with the exception of the expenses of his final illness which are a Class 4 debt.

If the decedent owed any back taxes to the state of Illinois, or if he owed property taxes to a county, township, city or village, those funds are 6th in priority of payment (755 ILCS 5/18-10).

CLASS 7: ALL OTHER CLAIMS

Any other debt or claim against the Estate is 7th in priority (755 ILCS 5/18-10).

There is no priority within the class, so if there is not enough money to pay all Class 7 debts, each will receive a pro rata share.

Illinois law requires that claims against the Probate Estate be paid in the given order. For example, suppose the decedent was single and left enough money to pay for his probate, the funeral, and his taxes (the first three classes) with $100,000 left over. If there are no other debts then the beneficiaries get the $100,000. But if the decedent was married with two minor children, the spouse could ask for support for herself and the children (Class 2). It could well be, that the support payment uses up all the money in the Estate and there is nothing left to pay any other beneficiary or any creditor.

✧ THERE IS A STATUTE OF LIMITATIONS ✧

There are federal and state laws that set time periods for pursuing a claim. Anyone who wishes to take Court action must do so within the time set by the given Statute of Limitation. For example, a law suit for the wrongful death of the decedent must be filed within two years of the death (740 ILCS 180/2).

There is a Statute of Limitations for a creditor to come forward and make a claim against the decedent's Estate for monies owed. The Personal Representative is required to publish notice of the death in a newspaper of general circulation for three successive weeks. The creditor has six months from the first day that notice was published or three months from the date he was given notice by mail (whichever is the later date) to file a claim with the Probate Court (755 ILCS 5/18-3).

But what if no one starts a Probate procedure? Illinois statute (755 ILCS 5/18-12(b)) imposes a two year statute of limitations from the date of the decedent's death. If a claim is not filed within two years after the death, the claim cannot be enforced against the Estate, the Personal Representative, or any of the beneficiaries.

There are exceptions to the two-year limit such as mortgages and federal claims and certain liens on the decedent's property. But, in general, if no one starts a Probate procedure and two years have passed from the date of death, the beneficiaries may be able to obtain possession of the decedent's assets free from creditor claims.

Some may be thinking that it may be a good idea to postpone Probate until two years have passed.

Read on before you decide to wait out the two years.

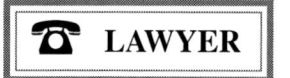

☎ LAWYER — **DECEDENT LEAVING CONSIDERABLE DEBT**

If the decedent died leaving much debt and no property, the solution is simple. No Probate — no one gets paid. But if the decedent had property and died owing more money than the property was worth, his heirs may decide that going through a Probate procedure is just not worth the effort, or they may decide to simply wait out the two year Statute of Limitation period and begin Probate at that time.

This may not be the best decision. Some creditors are tenacious and will use whatever legal strategy is available in order to be paid, including initiating Probate themselves. The person named as Executor in the decedent's Will loses his right to administer the Estate if he does not do so within 30 days of being notified of the death (755 ILCS 5/6-3). This leaves the door open for the creditor to ask to be appointed as Personal Representative.

As we will see in Chapter 6, a Personal Representative has much authority when conducting the Probate procedure. Family members may object to having a creditor as a Personal Representative, so there could be a Court battle over who has priority to be appointed as Personal Representative. Court battles are expensive, emotionally as well as financially. Before you decide to distance yourself from the Probate procedure, consult with an attorney experienced in Probate matters for an opinion about the best way to administer the Estate.

MONIES OWED TO THE DECEDENT

Suppose you owed money to the decedent. Do you need to pay that debt now that he is dead? That depends on whether there is some written document that says the debt is forgiven once the decedent dies. For example, suppose the decedent loaned you money to buy your home. If he left a Will saying that once he dies, your debt is forgiven, you do not need to make any more payments. If you signed a promissory note and mortgage at the time you borrowed the money from the decedent, the Personal Representative should sign the original promissory note **PAID IN FULL** and return the note to you. If the mortgage was recorded, the Personal Representative needs to have a Satisfaction of Mortgage recorded in the county where the property is located. You should receive the recorded Satisfaction for your records.

If you owed the decedent money and there is no Will, or if there is a Will, and no mention of forgiving the debt, then you still owe the money. Money borrowed from the decedent and his spouse needs to be repaid to the spouse. Money borrowed from the decedent only becomes an asset of the Estate of the decedent, meaning that you owe the money to the decedent's Estate. If you are one of the beneficiaries of the Estate, you may be able to deduct the money from your inheritance.

For example, suppose your father left $80,000 to be divided equally between you and your brother. If you owed your father $20,000, your father's Estate is really worth $100,000, with each child entitled to $50,000. Instead of paying the $20,000, you can agree to receive $30,000 and have the $20,000 debt forgiven. Your brother will receive the remaining $50,000.

Who Are The Beneficiaries? 5

A question that comes up early on is who is entitled to the property of the decedent. To answer the question, you first need to know how the property was titled (owned) as of the date of death.

There are three ways to own property. The decedent could have owned property jointly with another person, or in trust for another person; or the decedent could have owned property that was titled in his name only.

In general, upon the decedent's death:

> **Joint Property With Right of Survivorship** belongs to the surviving joint owner.
>
> **Trust Property** belongs to the beneficiary of the Trust.
>
> Property owned by the **decedent only** is inherited by the beneficiaries named in the Will. If there is no Will, the property goes to his heirs according to the Illinois Laws of Descent.
>
> **NOTE** ⇨ If the decedent was married, his spouse may have rights in his property.

This chapter describes each type of ownership in detail.

117

PROPERTY OWNED JOINTLY

Bank accounts, securities, motor vehicles, real property can all be owned jointly by two or more people. If one of the joint owners dies, then the survivor(s) continue to own their share of the property. Who owns the share belonging to the decedent depends on how the joint ownership was set up.

THE JOINT BANK ACCOUNT

When a bank account is opened, the depositors sign an agreement with the bank that states the terms and conditions of the account. If the account is opened in two or more names, the contract will say whether each depositor has authority to make a withdrawal, or whether two signatures are necessary. The statement will also say whether there is a right of survivorship. Unless the agreement with the bank states differently, it is presumed that each joint owner is an equal owner of the account and that there is a right of survivorship (765 ILCS 1005/2(a)).

Once an owner of a joint account dies, the surviving owner is free to withdraw all of the monies from the account without the need to go through any Probate procedure to get that money. If a joint bank account is held in three names, each with rights of survival, should one of the joint owners dies, any one of the remaining owners can withdraw all of the funds in the account.

It could become a race to the bank to take out all the money. But that would only serve to cause hard feelings. With such an arrangement, the remaining owners need to cooperate with each other and come to a joint decision about how to divide the account equitably.

JOINTLY HELD SECURITIES

You can determine whether the decedent owns a security alone or jointly with another by examining the face of the stock or bond certificate. If two names are printed on the certificate followed by a statement that the owners are "Joint Tenants With Right of Survivorship ("JTWRS")," the surviving owner can either cash in the security or ask the company to issue a new certificate in the name of the surviving owner (765 ILCS 1005/2(b)). You will need to forward a certified copy of the death certificate to the company and ask that they send you the necessary forms to make the change.

Each state has its own securities regulations. If a security held in two or more names, was registered or purchased in another state, and it does not indicate whether there is a right of survivorship, you need to contact the company to determine how the account was set up; i.e. with or without a right of survivorship.

If the decedent held his securities in a brokerage account, you need to check the monthly or quarterly brokerage statement to see if the account was owned jointly. Not all brokerage firms include the name of the joint owner on the brokerage statement, so you need to contact the firm to determine whether there is a surviving joint owner, or perhaps a beneficiary of the account.

Request a copy of the contract that is the basis of the account. The contract will show when the account was opened and the terms of the brokerage account.

JOINTLY OWNED MOTOR VEHICLE

If a motor vehicle is held jointly, the name of each owner is printed on the title to the motor vehicle. If one person dies, the other owns the car (765 ILCS 1005/2(e)). If you are the surviving joint owner, you can change title by taking the original title certificate and a certified copy of the death certificate to the **VEHICLE SERVICES DEPARTMENT** of the nearest Secretary of State facility. They will assist you with the necessary paper work to change title and registration to your name only. You may want to first call to determine the cost of making the change. You can get the address and telephone number of Secretary of State facilities from the Internet.

ILLINOIS SECRETARY OF STATE
http://www.sos.state.il.us/departments/vehicles

Illinois law (625 ILCS 5/3-114) requires the surviving owner to change title within 120 days of the death; however, it is important to change title as soon as you are able. You might be able to get a reduced insurance rate if there is only one person insured under the policy. Also, should you be involved in an accident, and title has officially been changed, there is no question that the Estate of the decedent is in any way liable for the accident.

MOTOR VEHICLE IN DECEDENT'S NAME ONLY

If the decedent's car was in his name only and he left a Will, the car goes to the beneficiaries named in the Will. If the decedent died without a Will, it is inherited by his next of kin as defined in the Illinois Laws of Descent and Distribution. See Chapter 6 for an explanation of how to transfer title to the motor vehicle.

REAL PROPERTY OWNED JOINTLY

The name of the owner of real property is printed on the front page of the deed. To determine whether the decedent owned the property jointly with another, you need to look at the last recorded deed. See Chapter 3 if you cannot locate the deed.

The top paragraph of the deed identifies the person who transferred the property to the current owner. That person is identified as the *Grantor*. For example:

> Grantor, ROBERT TRAYNOR, of LaSalle County, for and in consideration of $200,000 paid in hand, conveys and warrants to ALFRED CODY and ROBERT CODY **NOT AS TENANTS IN COMMON BUT AS JOINT TENANTS** the following described real estate . . .

Alfred and Robert are the *Grantees* and current owners of the property. Because the deed identifies them as Joint Tenants and NOT as Tenants In Common, there are rights of survivorship. Should one of the Grantees die, the surviving Joint Tenant will own the property 100%.

Nothing need be done to establish the ownership, however the decedent's name remains on the deed. If you are the surviving owner, you may want your attorney to prepare and record a document to let anyone who examines title to the property that your are now the sole owner. See chapter 6 for information about transferring real property.

WHO ARE THE BENEFICIARIES?

📄 DEED HELD AS TENANT IN COMMON

If a deed identifies the decedent and another as **TENANTS IN COMMON**, the decedent's share of the property belongs to whomever the decedent named as his beneficiary in his Will. If the decedent died without a Will, the Illinois Laws of Descent determine who inherits the decedent's share of the property. Generally, a Probate procedure will be necessary to transfer the decedent's share of the property to the proper beneficiary.

In Illinois, there is no implied right of survivorship. A deed must contain specific survivorship language such as **JOINT TENANTS, AND NOT AS TENANTS IN COMMON** otherwise the Grantees own the property as Tenants In Common (765 ILCS 1005/1).

☎ LAWYER — THE AMBIGUOUS DEED

Most deeds clearly state whether the joint owners of the property intend a surviving owner to inherit the decedent's share. But some deeds are not all that clear. For example, if the deed reads "**JOINT TENANTS**" and nothing more, depending on the circumstances surrounding the conveyance, it may be that a Court later determines that the surviving owner does not inherit the decedent's share.

If you have any question about how to interpret a deed, it is best to consult with an attorney.

DEED HELD AS HUSBAND AND WIFE

There are rights of survivorship for property owned by a married couple as **TENANTS BY THE ENTIRETY**. For example:
TODD AMES AND SUSAN AMES, husband and wife as TENANTS BY THE ENTIRETY

Should either spouse die, and providing they are married at the time of death, the surviving spouse owns the property 100%.

If the deed does not identify them as:
TENANTS BY THE ENTIRETY,
or does not say that they hold title as:
NOT AS TENANTS IN COMMON, BUT IN JOINT TENANCY,
then they hold title as **TENANTS IN COMMON** (765 ILCS 1005/1, 1005/1c).

☎ LAWYER — DIVORCED PRIOR TO DEATH

Under Illinois law real property owned by a married couple as: Tenants By The Entirety, or as
Joint Tenants and Not As Tenants In Common
upon their divorce becomes property owned by them as Tenants In Common (765 ILCS 1005/1c).

The Final Judgment should state who is to own the property after the divorce. However, if one of the parties dies before the deed to their joint property was transferred to the proper owner, you may need to consult with an attorney to have the property transferred to the proper beneficiary.

WHO ARE THE BENEFICIARIES?

📄 DEED WITH A LIFE ESTATE

A *Life Estate* interest in real property means that the person who owns the Life Estate has the right to live in that property until he dies. You can identify a Life Estate interest by examining the face of the deed. If somewhere on the face of the deed you see the phrase RESERVING A LIFE ESTATE to the deceased Grantor, then the Grantee now owns the property. For example, suppose the granting paragraph of the deed reads:

> The Grantor, LEONA SPAULDING
> of Kankakee County
> for good and valuable consideration
> Conveys and warrants to FRANK SPAULDING
> the following described real estate . . .
>
> **RESERVING A LIFE ESTATE TO LEONA SPAULDING**

Leona is the owner of the Life Estate. Frank owns the *Remainder Interest* in the property. Frank has no right to occupy the property during Leona's lifetime, but once she dies, he will own the property 100%. He will be free to take possession of the property or transfer it, as he sees fit.

As with a survivorship tenancy, nothing need be done to establish Frank's ownership of the property once Rose dies, however he may wish to have his attorney record an Affidavit to show anyone who is examining title to the property that he now owns the property.

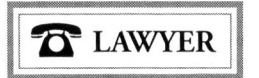

☎ LAWYER — THE OUT OF STATE DEED

The laws of the state or country where the property is located determine who inherits property within that state. If the decedent owned property in another state or country, regardless of whether he was a resident of Illinois, the laws of the state determine who inherits that property.

The laws of each state are similar, but not the same. Laws differ in how the deed needs to be worded in order to have a right of survivorship. Some states require the deed to specifically say there is a right of survivorship. In such states, a deed held as Joint Tenant with no reference to survivorship is a Tenancy In Common.

The rights of married couples vary significantly. In some states, a right of survivorship is created between a married couple merely by having the owners identified as "Husband and Wife." In other states, including Illinois, survivorship rights must be specifically stated.

If the decedent was married, and owned property in his name only, his surviving spouse may have rights in that property. That is the case in Community property states. In other states, a surviving spouse may have Dower rights or other statutory rights.

If the decedent owned property in another state, it is important to consult with an attorney in that state to determine who now owns the property.

CAUTION   THERE COULD BE A LATER DEED

The above discussion on the different types of ownership of real property assumes that you are in possession of the most recent, valid deed. The decedent could have signed another, later deed.

Before you come to a conclusion about who inherits the property it is advisable to have a title search by an attorney or a title insurance company to determine the owner of the property as of the decedent's date of death.

PROPERTY HELD IN TRUST

BANK/ SECURITY ACCOUNTS

If a bank account is held in the name of the decedent "in trust for" or "for the benefit of" someone, once the bank has a certified copy of the death certificate, the bank will turn over the account to the beneficiary. Such account is commonly referred to as a **Totten Trust Account** (760 ILCS 5/3). Similarly, if a securities account is held "in trust for" someone, upon receipt of the death certificate, that account becomes the property of the beneficiary. If the beneficiary of the account is a minor, the financial institution may refuse to transfer the funds without Court approval. See Chapter 7 for a discussion of a gift to minors.

BANK ACCOUNT HELD BY A TRUSTEE

If the bank or security account is registered in the name of the decedent "as Trustee under a Trust Agreement," that means the decedent was the Trustee of a Trust and the bank will turn over that account to the Successor Trustee of the Trust. Banks usually require a copy of the Trust Agreement or a Certificate that identifies the Successor Trustee, so the bank should be aware of the identity of the Successor Trustee. If the Trust was amended to name a different Successor Trustee, you need to present the bank with a copy of that amendment together with a certified copy of the death certificate.

MOTOR VEHICLE

If the motor vehicle is held in the name of the decedent "as Trustee," then the motor vehicle continues to be Trust property. The Successor Trustee will need to contact the Vehicle Services Department to have title changed to that of the Successor Trustee. The Successor Trustee will then dispose of the car according to the terms of the Trust Agreement.

REAL PROPERTY

If the decedent had a Trust and put real property that he owned into the Trust, the deed may read something like this:

> JOHN ZAMORA and MARIA ZAMORA, his wife,
> of LaSalle County, Illinois
> for consideration paid, grants to
> JOHN ZAMORA, **Trustee,**
> **or his successors in Trust, under the**
> **JOHN ZAMORA REVOCABLE TRUST AGREEMENT**
> DATED September 2, 2005
> the following described real property
> . . .

The death of the Trustee of a Trust does not change the ownership of the property. It remains in the Trust. The Trust document might say whether the person who takes John's place as Trustee (the Successor Trustee) should sell or keep the property or perhaps give it to a beneficiary. The Trust may give the Successor Trustee the right to decide what to do with the property. If you are a beneficiary of the Trust and are concerned about what the Successor Trustee will do with the property, it is best to consult with your attorney to learn about your rights under that Trust.

THE DEED OF TRUST

A Deed of Trust is very different from the above described deed. The Deed of Trust is essentially a mortgage. The owner of the property places title to the property with a Trustee as security for payment of monies owed to the lender. If the debt is not paid, then the Trustee (after proper foreclosure on the property) will deliver title to the property to the Beneficiary of the Deed of Trust, namely the lender.

PROPERTY IN DECEDENT'S NAME ONLY

If the decedent owned property that was in his name only (not jointly or in trust for someone), a Probate procedure may be necessary in order to transfer the property to the proper beneficiary. Who is entitled to the decedent's Probate Estate depends on whether he died with or without a valid Will. If he had a valid Will, the beneficiaries of his property are identified in the Will.

If he died without a valid Will, the Illinois Laws of Descent determine who inherits the decedent's Probate Estate and what percentage of the Probate Estate each heir is to receive once all the bills and costs of administering the Probate procedure are paid.

The law recognizes the right of the family to inherit the decedent's property. The law covers all possible relationships beginning with the decedent's spouse. But before we discuss the rights of the surviving spouse we need to consider whether the decedent had a marriage that is considered as being valid within state of Illinois.

BEING MARRIED IN ILLINOIS

To be married in Illinois means that a man and a woman have obtained a license to marry from the County Clerk, solemnized the marriage by a state or religious ceremony, and then had the Clerk register the marriage with Department of Public Health (750 ILCS 5/201). No one under the age of 16 is allowed to marry in Illinois. Parental consent is required for anyone who is 16 or 17. If the parent cannot be located, or if the parent refused to consent, the Court may order the Clerk to issue the license (750 ILCS 5/208).

Illinois law specifically prohibits the marriage of people:
- ☒ who are currently married to another person
- ☒ who are **ancestors** (parent, grandparents, etc.) or **descendants** (child, grandchild, etc.) of each other
- ☒ who are brother and sister, regardless of whether the relationship is by adoption of the half blood; i.e. they have only one parent in common
- ☒ who are aunt and nephew or uncle and niece, regardless of whether the relationship is by the whole or half blood
- ☒ who are first cousins, unless both parties are at least 50 years old; or if either party is permanently and irreversibly sterile (750 ILCS 5/212).

GOING OUT OF STATE WON'T WORK

Any resident of Illinois who goes out of state to enter into a marriage that is prohibited in Illinois will not have that marriage recognized in the state of Illinois, and vice versa. No marriage contracted in this state by someone living in another state, is valid if that marriage is prohibited in the other state (750 ILCS 5/216, 5/217).

THE COMMON LAW MARRIAGE

A Common Law marriage is one that has not been solemnized by ceremony. It is more than just living together. The couple must agree to live together as man and wife, and then publicly hold themselves out as being married; i.e., tell friends and family that they are married. Many states no longer recognize a Common Law marriage as being valid, and have passed laws to that effect. The state of Illinois does not recognize a Common Law marriage that was entered into in the state of Illinois after June 30, 1905 (750 ILCS 5/214).

Although Common Law marriages are no longer valid in the state of Illinois, they are not specifically prohibited. Illinois Courts have ruled that they will not recognize a Common Law marriage entered into in Illinois, but if the couple entered into the marriage in another state; and if that marriage is valid in that state, and the marriage is not prohibited under Illinois law, the marriage is considered to be valid here in Illinois (*Jambrone v. David*, 16 Ill.2d 32, 156 N.E.2d 569).

SAME SEX MARRIAGES

In 1998, the federal government passed the Defense of Marriage Act, saying that for purposes of federal law, marriage is a legal union between one man and one woman (28 U.S.C. 1738C). However, for purposes of state law, whether you can marry, who you can marry; and how you can marry, are determined by the laws of the state in which you live.

There is much variation state to state. California law gives *registered Domestic Partners* the same rights and responsibilities as a married couple. Vermont and Connecticut have approved same-sex *Civil Unions*. Massachusetts allows gay marriages. The Defense of Marriage Act also provides that no state is required to recognize the laws of another state as relating to same sex marriage. And this is the case in Illinois. Illinois law bans same sex marriages and will not recognize a marriage between those of the same gender regardless of whether that relationship is legal anywhere else (750 ILCS 5/213.1).

It is important to consult with an attorney if you have any question about the validity of the decedent's marriage.

THE LAWS OF DESCENT

If the decedent died *intestate*, i.e., without a Will, the state of Illinois provides one for him in the form of its **Laws of Descent and Distribution**. These laws are also referred to as the *Laws of Intestate Succession*. Once his debts, funeral expenses, and the cost of the Probate is paid, whatever is left (his *net Probate Estate*) is distributed as follows:

❖ DESCENDANT, NO SPOUSE

If the decedent was single and left descendants (child, grandchild, great-grandchild, etc.), his Net Probate Estate is inherited by his descendants. If he had two or more children, all who survive him, each child is entitled to an equal share of his Estate (755 ILCS 5/2-1(b)).

If a child of the decedent dies before the decedent, the share intended for that child goes to the descendants of the deceased child in equal shares. For example, suppose the decedent was single with four children, Ann, Barry, Carl, David. If he died without a Will, each child gets 25% of his Net Probate Estate.

CHILD WITHOUT DESCENDANTS DIES BEFORE DECEDENT

If Ann dies before her father, leaving no descendants, Barry, Carl and David divide the Estate between them. Each gets one third of the Net Probate Estate.

CHILD WITH DESCENDANTS DIES BEFORE DECEDENT

Suppose instead that only Carl and David survived their father. If Ann died leaving no children and Barry died leaving 2 children, then the Estate is divided into 3 shares — one for each surviving child (Carl and David) and one share for Barry's children, who split their share equally.

The legal term to describe this method of distributing property is called ***per stirpes.***

✧ MARRIED

If the decedent was married, without any descendants, his surviving spouse inherits his entire Probate Estate.

If he was married and was survived by descendants, the spouse gets half of the net Probate Estate. The other half goes to his descendants, per stirpes (755 ILCS 5/2-1(a)).

✧ SINGLE, NO DESCENDANT

If the decedent was single without descendants, but he had a surviving parent and/or brother and/or sister, his Estate is divided into equal shares, one for each parent and one for each brother and sister. If one of his parents is deceased, the surviving parent gets a double share. If a sibling (brother or sister) is deceased but with surviving children, that share goes to the children, per stirpes (755 ILCS 5/2-1(d)).

There is no distinction for relatives of half blood, i.e., if the decedent had one brother from the same set of parents, and a sister with the same mother and a different father, both brother and sister inherit an equal share of the decedent's Estate.

SURVIVING GRANDPARENT, AUNT, UNCLE OR COUSIN

If the decedent had no surviving parent, brother, sister, nephew or niece, the Estate is divided in half, with half going to the decedent's maternal grandparents, in equal shares, per stirpes and the other half going to the decedent's paternal grandparents, in equal shares, per stirpes.

Should there be surviving relatives on one side of the family only, the entire Estate is inherited by that side of the family (755 ILCS 5/2-1(e)).

We could give an example of how the Estate is distributed if the decedent is survived only by descendants of his grandparents, but we thought you might enjoy a puzzle instead:

Winston died intestate leaving $100,000. His only relatives are his mother's sister, Aunt Susie, and her children, Ramona and Abigail and a first cousin Elvis, on his father's side. How much does each relative receive?

You can check your answer by visiting the puzzle section of the Eagle Publishing Company Web site.
http://www.eaglepublishing.com

THE STATE: HEIR OF LAST RESORT

As explained in Chapter 3, unclaimed property goes to the state, so if a person dies without a Will, and no relations, his Probate Estate is "inherited" by the state of Illinois. Any real property owned by the decedent becomes the property of the county where the property is located. Any personal property (bank accounts, securities, etc.) goes to the county where the decedent lived. If the decedent was not a resident of Illinois, it goes to the county where the property is located (755 ILCS 5/2-1 (h)).

CAUTION IT ISN'T ALL THAT SIMPLE

The explanation in this book of the Laws of Descent is abridged. There is much more to the law. Unless the descent is straight forward, with the decedent leaving a surviving spouse and/or children (all who survive him), it is best to consult with an attorney before you decide who is entitled to inherit the decedent's intestate property.

THE RIGHTS OF A CHILD

THE ADOPTED CHILD

An adopted person who was a minor at the time of adoption, or who lived with the adoptive parent prior to his 18th birthday, has the same right to inherit property under the Laws of Descent from his adoptive parents as does a natural child. The adopted child has no right to inherit from his natural parents, with the exception of the natural parent who is married to the adoptive parent. For example, if a child loses a parent and is later adopted by a step-parent, the child has the right to inherit from his natural parents and from his adoptive parent as well.

An adopted person who was an adult at the time of the adoption keeps his right to inherit property from his natural parents. If the child was adopted after the age of 18, and did not live with the adoptive parents prior to that time, the adoptive child is not considered a child for the purpose of inheriting property from any member of his adoptive family other than from his parents.

For example, if the decedent was the adoptive grandparent of someone adopted after the age of 18, unless the grandparent left a specific gift for that adopted person in his Will, the adopted person has no right to inherit anything from the adoptive grandparent in the state of Illinois. This law was adopted by the Illinois legislature in 1997 and applies only to Wills drafted after 1/1/98 (755 ILCS 5/2-4).

THE AFTERBORN CHILD

A child who was conceived prior to the decedent's death, and born to the surviving spouse after the death, has the same right to inherit as any other natural child of the decedent (755 ILCS 5/2-3).

We discussed the rights of children when the parent dies without a Will, but suppose the decedent left a Will and did not include anything for a child. Is that child entitled to some part of the decedent's Estate? The answer is "no," provided the decedent left a valid Will clearly stating that it was the decedent's wish not to give anything to the child. But suppose the Will was drafted before the child was born and the decedent did not change his Will to include the child. In such case, the child has the right to inherit as much of the decedent's Estate as if he died without a Will (755 ILCS 5/4-10).

THE NON-MARITAL CHILD

A child born out of wedlock has the same rights to inherit from his/her natural father as does one born in wedlock, provided any one of the following are true:

- ☑ He married the mother after the birth, and acknowledged the child as his own — or —
- ☑ He acknowledged the child as his own — or —
- ☑ His paternity is established by a Court.

If the decedent denied he was the child's father, it will take a Court procedure to establish (or disprove) paternity. The Court will require clear and convincing evidence that he is the father (755 ILCS 5/2-2 (h)).

NO SHARE FOR FATHER OF A NON-MARITAL CHILD

Under the Illinois Laws of Descent, the father of a non-marital child has no right to inherit from the Estate of that child unless he:

⇨ acknowledged the child as his own AND
⇨ established a parental relationship with the child AND
⇨ provided financial support to the child
(755 ILCS 5/2-2)

☎ LAWYER **NO SHARE FOR NEGLECTFUL PARENT**

If a minor or dependent child dies owning property, his parents are entitled to inherit the property — but not if they neglected their parental duties. A parent who has wilfully neglected or failed to support a minor or dependent child for a year or more prior to the child's death may have the amount inherited by Will or under the Illinois Laws of Descent reduced, or eliminated altogether, by the Probate Court (755 ILCS 5/2-6.5).

If you wish to challenge a parent's right to inherit from a minor or dependent child, you will need to employ an attorney to bring the matter to the attention of the Court.

WHO DIED FIRST?

Sometimes it happens that two family members die simultaneously, and no one knows who died first. For example, suppose a husband and wife die together in a car crash, how is the property distributed in that case?

If no provision was made by the decedent for a simultaneous death, then Illinois statute (755 ILCS 5/3-1) provides for an orderly distribution of their respective Estates. According to the statute, each person will be assumed to have survived the other and the property of each distributed in that manner.

PROCEEDS OF A LIFE INSURANCE POLICY
Suppose the husband is insured, with his wife as the beneficiary of his life insurance policy. The proceeds of the policy will be distributed as if the wife died before her husband. The proceeds will be given to the alternate beneficiary named in the policy. If no alternate beneficiary was named, the proceeds of the policy will go to the insured party (in this case, the husband).

JOINTLY OWNED PROPERTY
Property owned jointly by the couple, with no provision for who is to inherit the property should they both die, is divided with half going to the Estate of the husband and the other half to the Estate of the wife. If they each have a Will, the husband's half is distributed according to his Will and the wife's half according to her Will. If they die without a Will, each half is distributed according to the Illinois Laws of Descent.

> **Special Situation**: NO SHARE FOR KILLER

Under Illinois law anyone who is found guilty of the intentional and unjustified murder of the decedent is prohibited from profiting from the crime. Property that the killer would have inherited as a beneficiary of the decedent's Will or according to the Illinois Laws of Descent, will be distributed as if the killer died before the decedent.

Upon a Court determination of guilt, property that was owned by the decedent and the killer, or accessory, as Joint Property with Right of Survivorship becomes a Tenancy-In-Common, insofar as the killer and the decedent are concerned. Any other person who is a joint owner of the property, remains a joint owner.

Similarly, if the killer is a beneficiary of the decedents life insurance policy or annuity, whoever is named as alternate beneficiary will get the insurance proceeds. If no alternate beneficiary is named, the insurance proceeds become the property of the decedent's Estate (755 ILCS 5/2-6).

WHEN TO CHALLENGE THE WILL

It is not uncommon for a family member to be unhappy with the way the decedent willed his property. If you are tempted to challenge a Will, first consider whether the Will is valid under Illinois law. A Will is enforceable in Illinois, if at the time the decedent made the Will:

➢ he was 18 years of age or older
➢ he was of sound mind and memory
(755 ILCS 5/4-1).

Illinois Courts have ruled that "sound mind and memory" means that when the decedent made his the Will, he knew:

⇨ what he was doing (namely, making a Will)
⇨ what property he owned
⇨ which of his relatives would, under ordinary circumstances, expect to inherit his property (*Anthony v. Anthony*, 20 Ill.2d 584 (1960)).

☒ THE UNWITNESSED WILL

The first step in the Probate procedure is to have the Probate Court determine whether the Will presented is valid. If the Will is in writing and signed by the Will maker in the presence of at least two credible witnesses, there should be no problem in having the Will accepted into Probate. But suppose the decedent wrote out a Will in his own hand and signed it with no one present? A Will written in the Will maker's hand is called a *holographic Will*. Illinois law requires that a Will be in writing and signed in the presence of two witness, so the Probate Court will not accept an unwitnessed holographic Will into Probate (755 ILCS 5/4-3).

Not all states refuse to recognize a holographic Will. If the decedent died in Illinois but his primary residence was in another state, you need to check whether the Probate Court of that state might decide that the Will is valid.

But the problem with a holographic Will, in this or any other state, is its authenticity. Because no one saw the decedent sign the Will, it is hard to determine whether the Will was written by the decedent or is a forgery. If all the decedent left was a holographic Will that he signed as a resident of another state, you need to consult with an attorney experienced in Probate matters to determine whether the Will can be admitted into Probate in that state.

☒ THE WILL WITNESSED BY A BENEFICIARY

Neither of the witnesses should be a beneficiary of the Will unless there are two other, independent, disinterested witnesses. Under Illinois law, if there are only two witnesses, one of whom is a beneficiary of the Will, or whose spouse is a beneficiary of the Will, the most that beneficiary (or his spouse) can inherit is what they would have received had the decedent died without a Will (755 ILCS 5/4-6).

But a Will is not invalid because a beneficiary of the Will, witnesses the Will. It just means that the beneficiary may not be entitled to receive that gift. Of course if the beneficiary of the Will (or his spouse) are the only beneficiaries of the Will, the Court may find that the entire is Will invalid. In such case, a prior valid Will can be admitted to Probate. If there is no prior Will, the property will be distributed according to the Illinois Laws of Descent.

The reason Illinois law has laws regarding a beneficiary of the Will who is also a witness is that of *undue influence*. Undue influence occurs whenever someone exerts such pressure on the Will maker so that he is not acting according to his own free will. But undue influence is not easily proven. Courts have ruled that the person who challenges the Will on the basis of undue influence needs to prove:

⇨ the Will maker had a trusting and confidential relationship with the beneficiary of the Will, AND

⇨ the beneficiary was dominant and the Will maker was dependent on the beneficiary, AND

⇨ the beneficiary arranged to have the Will prepared (*Herbolsheimer v Herbolsheimer*, 361 N.E.2d 134, Ill.App. 1977).

☒ THE VERBAL WILL

Picture a death bed scene. The elderly gentleman is surrounded by several family members. In a whisper, just audible enough to be heard, he says: "Even though I am a wealthy man, I never got around to making a Will. You all have been good to me, but I did want my entire fortune to go to my nephew, Robert. He has been like a son to me."

Do you think Robert can inherit his Uncle's Estate? Not in Illinois unless:

⇨ Someone writes down his uncles's wishes, and
⇨ The uncle acknowledges that this is his Will, and
⇨ The uncle signs the Will or directs someone to sign the Will on his behalf, and
⇨ Two people sign the Will as witnesses
(755 ILCS 5/4-3).

Considering that the uncle's relatives will probably inherit the fortune under the Illinois Laws of Descent, it is doubtful that Robert is in danger of becoming wealthy at any time in the near future.

WHEN TO CHALLENGE A WILL

If you can prove the decedent was under 18 when he signed the Will, you have it made. Challenging the Will on other grounds may be difficult — especially if the Will was prepared by the decedent's attorney, who will, no doubt, testify that the Will maker's mind was perfectly clear when he signed the document; and that he signed it of his own free will. But difficult is not impossible. If you are concerned about the validity of the Will, it is important to consult with an attorney experienced in Probate litigation.

☒ THE WILL THAT IS CONTRARY TO LAW

Sometimes a person who is of sound mind makes a Will that has the effect of giving a spouse or a minor child less than they would otherwise receive under Illinois law. One such example is that of Nancy. Hers was not an easy life. She worked long hours as a waitress. She divorced her hard drinking first husband. The final judgment gave her their home, some securities, and sole custody of their son, Richard. After the divorce, Nancy had her attorney prepare a Will leaving all she owned to her son.

Some years later she met and married Harry, a chef at the restaurant where she worked. He moved into her home and they later had a daughter. Richard was 19, and his half-sister 12, when Nancy died after a lengthy battle with cancer.

Nancy did not leave much — her car, her home, and the securities worth about $100,000, all were in Nancy's name only. Just before she died, Nancy gave $10,000 to her son to pay for his room and board at college. At that time she told Richard that she had not changed her Will because she wanted him to have all she owned. She said Harry had a good job and she was sure he would take good care of his daughter.

No sooner was the funeral over when Richard came in and demanded that Harry vacate his mother's home. Harry was furious and went to his attorney.

"I was a good husband to Nancy, supporting and taking care of her all during her long illness. It was me, and not her son who was at her side when she died. Don't I have any rights? And what about my daughter? Doesn't she have any rights? "

"She sure does. Illinois law provides that if a child is born after a Will is made, that child is entitled to inherit as much as she would have inherited if her parent died without a Will. If Nancy died without a Will, half her Estate would have gone to her two children. That means your daughter is entitled to a quarter of Nancy's Estate (755 ILCS 5/4-10)."

"But what about the $10,000 she gave to Richard just before she died? Shouldn't my daughter get her share of that money?"

"Nancy was free to make a gift of her property at any time prior to her death. That gift does not count as part of her son's inheritance unless Nancy signed some document saying that the gift was an advancement of his inheritance (755 ILCS 5/2-5)."

"And what about my rights?"

As for your rights, Illinois law (750 ILCS 10/4(a)(3)) allows you to *waive* (give up) your rights in your spouse's Estate. Did you sign any premarital agreement giving up any or all of your rights?"

"Absolutely not!"

"In that case, Illinois law (755 ILCS 5/2-8) gives you the right to renounce the Will that Nancy wrote. If you do, you are entitled to one third of all of her property. You and your daughter might also be entitled to be paid support from Nancy's Estate while Probate is being conducted. How much you receive will be up to the judge. In addition you may be entitled to a Statutory Custodial Claim for the nursing care you gave to your wife during the last three years of her life. Again its up to the judge to set the amount of the award. But it could be significant."

"Sounds good to me."

"As for the homestead, even though it was in Nancy's name only, Illinois law (755 ILCS 5/20-1 (b)) provides that you are entitled to continue to live in your home, unless Nancy specifically stated in her Will that the house was to go to her son."

"No, the Will said that all of her Estate was to go to Richard. Nothing was specifically said about the house."

"In that case, then unless the court finds that the house must be sold to pay Nancy's debts, you can remain there. However if you do, the value of the home will be included as part of your share of Nancy's Estate. If the value of the home is more than half of Nancy's Estate, you will need to pay the difference to Richard and your daughter."

The judge did grant Harry a Statutory Custodial Claim, and support payments for her daughter while Probate was being conducted.

There was little left for Richard after:
- $$ funeral expenses $$ attorney's fees
- $$ Nancy's medical bills $$ costs of probate
- $$ Harry's Custodial claim and share of the inheritance
- $$ support payment for Nancy's daughter during Probate and her share of the inheritance.

Richard did not fare as well as his mother intended. All that Richard inherited was his share of the house which was a quarter of the proceeds of the sale.

And he didn't get that until it was all sold at the end of the year.

No doubt Nancy did not understand what would happen to her Estate once she passed on. The Will she left did not accomplish her goal of providing for her son. All it did was cause turmoil and an irreparable rift between Harry and Richard. Had she been advised about Illinois law, she could have held title to her house, car and securities jointly with her son. Had she done so, those items would not have been part of her Probate Estate. Her son would have owned them upon Nancy's death.

But the moral of the story, for the purpose of this discussion, is that if you believe that the decedent's Will is not valid or is not drafted according to Illinois law, then you need to consult with an attorney experienced in Probate matters to determine your legal rights under that Will.

Getting Possession Of The Property 6

Knowing who is entitled to receive the decedent's property is one thing. Getting that property is another. As explained in the previous chapter if the decedent held property jointly with right of survivor, or in trust for someone, the property now belongs to the joint owner or beneficiary. If it is personal property such as a bank account or a security, the beneficiary can usually get possession of the property by giving a certified copy of the death certificate to the financial institution.

If the decedent had real or personal property in his name only, or if he held property as a Tenant In Common, then some sort of Probate proceeding may be necessary in order to transfer ownership to the proper beneficiary. The assistance of an attorney may be required should a full Probate proceeding be necessary, but there are many items that can be transferred without legal assistance. This chapter explains how to get possession of those items.

The chapter also contains an explanation of the different kinds of Probate procedures and when it is appropriate to use that procedure.

DISTRIBUTING PERSONAL EFFECTS

Too often, the first person to discover the body will help himself to the decedent's *personal effects* (clothing, jewelry, appliances, electrical equipment, cameras, books, stamp or coin collection, household items and furnishing, etc.). Unless that person is the decedent's sole beneficiary, such action is unconscionable, if not illegal.

As explained on Page 107, the decedent's spouse, or if no spouse, his children are entitled to keep his clothing, family bible, school books, family pictures and other Exempt Property free of any creditor's claim (735 ILCS 5/12-1003). In all other cases, the personal effects should be given to the person appointed as the Personal Representative to be distributed according to the decedent's Will, or if no Will, according to the Illinois Laws of Descent.

If no Probate proceeding is necessary, his next of kin, as determined by the Illinois Laws of Descent, need to divide all of the personal effects among themselves in approximately equal proportions. Most personal effects have little, if any, monetary value. Furniture may be worth less than it costs to ship. In such case, the beneficiaries may decide to donate the personal property to the decedent's favorite charity.

What's Equal?

The decedent's Will may direct that the decedent's personal property be divided equally between two or more beneficiaries. The problem with the term "equal" is that people have different ideas of what "equal" means. Unless there is clear evidence that the decedent's Will meant something else, "equal" refers to the monetary value of the item and not to the number of items received.

For example, to divide the decedent's personal effects equally, one beneficiary may receive an expensive item of jewelry and another beneficiary may receive several items whose overall value is approximately equal to that single piece of jewelry.

When distributing personal effects there needs to be cooperation and perhaps compromise, or else bitter arguments might arise over items of little monetary value. One such argument occurred when an elderly woman died who was rich only in her love for her five children and ten grandchildren. After the funeral, the children gathered in their mother's apartment. Each child had his/her own furnishings and no need for anything in the apartment. They agreed to donate all of their mother's personal effects to a local charity with the exception of a few items of sentimental value.

Each child took some small item as a remembrance — a handkerchief, a large platter that their mother used to serve family dinners, a doily their mother crocheted. Things went smoothly until it came to her photograph album. Frank, the youngest sibling, said, "I'll take this." Marie objected saying "But there are pictures in that album that I want." Frank retorted, "You already took all the pictures Mom had on her dresser."

The argument went downhill from there. Unsettled sibling rivalries boiled over, fueled by the hurt of the loss that they were all experiencing. It almost came to blows when the eldest settled the argument: "Frank you make copies of all of the photos in the album for Marie. Marie, you make copies of all of the pictures that you took and give them to Frank. This way you both will have a complete set of Mom's pictures. And while you're at it, make copies for the rest of us."

NON-PROBATE TRANSFERS

A ***non-Probate transfer*** is a transfer of the decedent's property without the need for Probate. For example, if the decedent had a bank account in his name only with instruction to "Pay On Death" to someone, all the beneficiary need do is produce a death certificate and proper identification, and the bank will turn over the property to him.

Securities that are held jointly with someone, or with instructions to "Transfer On Death" to a named beneficiary, can be transferred to that beneficiary in the same manner (815 ILCS 10/9).

MOTOR VEHICLE OWNED JOINTLY

As explained in chapter 5, in Illinois, a car that is owned jointly by two people has rights of survivorship unless title to the car indicates otherwise. The surviving owner, is required to remove the decedent's name from the title within 120 days of the death (625 ILCS 5/3-114, 765 ILCS 1005/2(e)).

Surviving joint owners and surviving spouses do not need to pay vehicle registration fees until the current registration expires.

TRANSFERRING THE MOTOR VEHICLE

TRANSFERRING THE JOINTLY OWNED CAR
If you are the surviving joint owner of a car, you can transfer title by going to the nearest Driver's Services Department and completing form VSD-190 **APPLICATION FOR VEHICLE TITLE AND REGISTRATION**. You will need to take a certified copy of the death certificate and the original title showing joint ownership.

Before going to Driver Services you might want to call to determine the cost of the transfer and what other information they might require: (800) 252-8980. Out of state call (312) 792-1010.

You can change title by mail by calling for the necessary form and then returning the completed application, together with a check or money order, to:

> Office of the Secretary of State
> Vehicle Input Audit Section
> 424 Howlett Building
> 501 S. Second Street
> Springfield, IL 62756

TRANSFERRING THE CAR IN THE DECEDENT'S NAME ONLY
If the car was titled in the decedent's name only and he owned personal property, worth no more than $100,000, the car can be transferred by means of a **SMALL ESTATE AFFIDAVIT**. The Small Estate Affidavit is described later in this Chapter, however, you can obtain the form at your local Driver Services Department or you can call or write to the office of the Secretary of State and they will mail you a copy. The Affidavit is also available on the Internet.

> **DRIVER SERVICES DEPARTMENT**
> http://www.cyberdriveillinois.com

TRANSFER BY PERSONAL REPRESENTATIVE

If Probate is necessary, the Personal Representative will transfer title to the car as part of that procedure. The Letters issued by the Court give the Personal Representative authority to transfer title to the proper beneficiary. The Personal Representative will transfer the car according to the terms of the Will. If the Will makes a ***specific gift*** of the car, the Personal Representative will transfer the car to that person. If there was no mention of the car in the decedent's Will, it goes to the ***residuary beneficiaries*** under the Will, i.e., those who inherit the **Residuary Estate** (whatever is left once the bills, taxes, costs of administration are paid and special gifts distributed. If the decedent did not have a Will, the car goes to the his heirs as determined by the Illinois Laws of Descent and Distribution.

TRANSFER WHEN MORE THAN ONE BENEFICIARY
If there is more than one person who has the right to inherit the car, they all can take title to the car. That may not be a practical thing to do since only one person can drive the car at any given time and if one gets into an accident, they all can be held liable. The better route is for the beneficiaries to agree to have one person take title to the car. The person taking title will need to compensate the others for their share of the car. In such case the beneficiaries need to come to an agreement as to the value of the car.

DETERMINING THE VALUE OF THE CAR
Cars are valued in different ways. The *collateral* value of the car is the value that banks use to evaluate the car for purposes of making a loan to the owner of the car. If you were to trade in a car for the purpose of purchasing a new one, the car dealer would offer you its *wholesale* value.

Were you to purchase that same car from a car dealer, he would price it at its *retail* or *fair market value*. Usually the retail price is highest, wholesale is lowest and its collateral value is somewhere in between.

You can call your local bank to get the collateral value of the car. It may be more difficult to obtain the wholesale value because the amount of money a dealer is willing to pay depends on the value of the new car that you are purchasing. You can determine the car's retail value by looking at comparable used car advertisements in the local newspaper.

Rather than going through the effort of determining these three values, you can use your Internet search engine to look up the Kelley Blue Book Value. The Web site gives Low, Average and High Blue Book Values which correspond to the wholesale, collateral and retail values.

Once the fair market value of the car is determined, the beneficiary who takes the car will be considered to have received that value as part of his inheritance. If none of the beneficiaries want the car, the Personal Representative will sell it and add the proceeds to the amount distributed to the beneficiaries.

It is a good idea to limit the use of the car until it is sold or transferred to the beneficiary. If the decedent's car is involved in an accident before the car is transferred to the new owner, the decedent's Estate may be liable for the damage. Having adequate insurance on the car may save the Estate from monetary loss, but a pending lawsuit could delay Probate and prevent any money from being distributed to the beneficiaries until the lawsuit is settled.

TRANSFERRING ALL-TERRAIN VEHICLES

Motorcycles that are operated on public streets are registered and titled in the same manner as any other motor vehicle. Off-highway motorcycles and All-terrain vehicles are titled, but not registered, with the Vehicle Services Department. You will need to transfer title to the decedent's Off-highway motorcycle or All-terrain vehicle at your nearest Vehicle Services Department.

TAXES ARE DUE ON THE TRANSFER

The state of Illinois imposes a **Motor Vehicle Use Tax** on the transfer of motor vehicles. You will need to complete Form RUT-50 and submit proof of tax payment before the Secretary of State will issue new title or registration. The tax form is in multiple parts, so you cannot download it from the Internet, but you can get the form from Driver Services, or from the Illinois Department of Revenue.

You can get a copy of RUT-50 by calling the Department of Revenue 24 hour Forms Order Line at (800) 356-6302, or by writing to: ILLINOIS DEPARTMENT OF REVENUE
P.O. Box 19010
Springfield, IL 62794-9010

CANCELING THE DRIVER'S LICENSE/IDENTIFICATION CARD

It is a good idea to turn in the decedent's driver's license or Identification Card at the same time you transfer title to his car. You can do this by writing "Deceased" across the driver's licence Identification Card and giving it to the **DRIVER SERVICES DEPARTMENT.** The Department will take the decedent off of their mailing list. This will assist the Department in preventing others from using the decedent's name for fraudulent purposes.

TRANSFERRING THE MOBILE HOME

A mobile home that is motorized and not permanently attached to real property is considered to be personal property. Like any motor vehicle it is titled and registered with the Illinois Secretary of State. The beneficiary of the mobile home will need to have it titled and registered in the same manner as just described.

A manufactured/mobile home that is permanently attached to a parcel of land, must be registered with Supervisor of Assessments or the County Assessor (35 ILCS 515/1, 515/4). Manufactured/mobile homes are subject to the Mobile Home Local Services Tax. If you inherit the decedent's home you need to check to see whether those taxes are current. If you wish to move the manufactured/mobile home to a new location, the transporting company will need to obtain a permit from the County Treasurer certifying that taxes on the mobile home are current; i.e., there are no outstanding taxes due.

If you move the home to a trailer park, the owner of the park will, within five days, register the mobile home with the County Assessor. If you are moving the home to a private location, you need to register the home with the Supervisor of Assessments or the County Assessor within 30 days of the move (35 ILCS 515/11).

If you inherited a mobile home and the land under the home, you will need to register your ownership of the manufactured/mobile home with the County Assessor, and transfer the land itself as discussed later in this Chapter.

Special Situation ▷ **TRANSFERRING THE LEASED CAR**

The leased car is not an asset of the Estate because the decedent did not own the car. The decedent was obligated to pay the balance of the monies owed on the lease agreement, so the car is a liability to the Estate. The Personal Representative needs to work out an agreement with the company to either assign the lease to someone who agrees to pay the balance of the lease — or have the Estate pay off the lease by purchasing the car under the terms of the lease agreement.

Some lenders will allow the lease to be assigned provided the Estate remains liable for the balance of payment. In such cases, it is better to have the car refinanced and have the original lease paid in full.

If the remaining payments exceed the current market value of the car, there may be a temptation to hand the keys over to the leasing company. This may not be the best strategy, because the leasing company can sell the car and then sue the Estate for the balance of the monies owed. If the decedent had no assets or if the only assets he had are creditor proof, simply returning the car may be an option. But if the decedent's Estate has assets available to pay the balance of the lease payments, the Personal Representative needs to arrange to have the car transferred in a way that releases the Estate from all further liability.

TRANSFERRING WATERCRAFT

All watercraft operated on Illinois waterways (other than sailboards) must be registered with the Illinois Department of Natural Resources (625 ILCS 45/3-1).

JOINTLY OWNED BOAT
If the decedent owned the boat jointly with survivorship rights, the surviving owner is required to apply for a certificate in his name, or in the name of whoever he wishes to own the boat.

Within 120 days of date of death, the surviving joint owner needs to deliver the following to the Department of Natural Resources:
- ☑ the last Certificate of Title (if available)
- ☑ a certified copy of the death certificate
- ☑ an application for a new Certificate of Title

(625 ILCS 45/3A-15).

You can get an application for the Certificate of Title by calling (800) 382-1696. Out of state, call (217) 557-0180; or by writing to: Department of Natural Resources
Watercraft Registration
One Natural Way
Springfield, IL 62702-1271

or you can download the Application from the Internet.

ILLINOIS DEPARTMENT OF NATURAL RESOURCES
http//www.dnr.state.il.us

TRANSFER BY PERSONAL REPRESENTATIVE
The Personal Representative can transfer the decedent's watercraft at any time prior to closing the Estate. He will do so as above described, but he will send a certified copy of his Letters instead of the death certificate.

TRANSFER BY SMALL ESTATE AFFIDAVIT

If Probate is not necessary, whoever inherits the watercraft can transfer the boat by sending an application within 120 days of the death, together with a Small Estate Affidavit to the Department of Natural Resources (625 ILCS 45/3A-15(b))).

The procedure for transferring watercraft by Affidavit is described in detail at the Department of Natural Resources Web site.

The Small Estate Affidavit and other documents that may be needed to make the transfer can be downloaded from the Department Web site. If you do not have Internet access, you can call the Department at (800) 382-1696. Out of state, call (217) 557-0180.

TAXES ARE DUE ON THE TRANSFER

The state of Illinois imposes a **Watercraft Use Tax** on the transfer of watercraft. You will need to complete Form RUT-75 and submit proof of tax payment to the Department of Natural Resources before your watercraft registration will be issued. You can get this form by calling the Department of Revenue 24 hour Forms Order Line at (800) 356-6302.

No tax need be paid if the decedent made a gift of the boat to his surviving spouse, however proof of this exemption will need to be given to the Department of Natural Resources.

TRANSFERRING THE SNOWMOBILE

A snowmobile that is operated on private property only, does not need to be registered with the Department of Natural Resource, but if it is operated anywhere else in Illinois it must have a Registration Expiration Decal and Certificate of Number. Regardless of whether the snowmobile is transferred to a beneficiary, or sold, the new owner must, within 15 days of the transfer, apply for an Illinois title or registration to the Department. The application procedure is much the same as explained on the previous page. As with the transfer of watercraft, the new owner must pay a Use Tax, or submit proof that no tax is due, before the Department will register the vehicle (625 ILCS 40/3-1, 40/3-11).

TRANSFERRING AIRCRAFT

As explained in Chapter 3, the Division of Aeronautics of the Illinois Department of Transportation is in charge of the registration of aircraft that is based in, or primarily used within, the state. If the decedent owned an aircraft, the Personal Representative will need to transfer title to the proper beneficiary. There is an Aircraft Use Tax on the transfer of the plane; however there is no tax on a gift made to the surviving spouse as part of the Probate proceeding (35 ILCS 157/10-15).

The new owner will need to arrange for his own aircraft registration with the Illinois Department of Transportation. He can call them at (800) 554-0247 for information about what is needed in order to register an aircraft in the state of Illinois, or he can download the necessary applications from the Internet.

THE ILLINOIS DEPARTMENT OF TRANSPORTATION
http://www.dot.state.il.us/aero/

THE FEDERAL INCOME TAX REFUND

Any refund due to the decedent under a joint federal income tax return filed by his surviving spouse will be sent to the surviving spouse. If the decedent's Personal Representative filed the final return, the refund check will be sent to him to be deposited to the Estate account.

If the decedent was single and no Probate proceeding is necessary, whoever is entitled to the decedent's Estate is entitled to the refund check. If you are the beneficiary of the decedent's Estate, you can obtain the refund by filing IRS form 1310 along with the decedent's final income tax return (the 1040).

You can obtain form 1310 from the decedent's accountant, or if he did not have an accountant and you wish to file yourself, you can call the IRS at (800) 829-3676 to obtain the form.

You can download instructions, publications and forms from the Internal Revenue Service by going to the **FORMS AND PUBLICATIONS** section of their Web site.

INTERNAL REVENUE SERVICE
http://www.irs.gov/

The Personal Representative does not need to file form 1310 because once he files the decedent's final income tax return, any refund will be forwarded to him. Similarly, it is not necessary for the surviving spouse who filed a joint return to file form 1310.

THE ILLINOIS INCOME TAX REFUND

An Illinois income tax is imposed on the income earned or received by the decedent within the state regardless of whether he was a resident of the state (35 ILCS 5/201). There is a basic exemption of $2,000, so a state income tax return does not need to be filed unless he earned more that amount.

The decedent's final Illinois income tax return needs to be filed at the same time the federal income tax return is filed (35 ILCS 5/505). If the decedent was married, his spouse can file a joint return. If a Probate proceeding is necessary, the Personal Representative has the responsibility of filing the final tax return. If Probate is not necessary, the decedent's next of kin can file the final return.

If you have any question about filing the decedent's final return, you can call the Illinois Department of Revenue at (217) 785-7701, or visit their Web site.
http://www.revenue.state.il.us

THE TAX REFUND

Claims for an income tax refund must be filed with the Department of Revenue within three years from the day the return was filed, or one year after the tax was paid — whichever is later (35 ILCS 5/911). If the decedent was not married, and the Personal Representative filed the final return, the refund check will be sent to him to be deposited into the Estate account. If Probate is not necessary and the refund check (or any other check) is in the name of the decedent, you can deposit it into the decedent's bank account. You can get the money in the decedent's account by using whatever Probate procedure is appropriate. If all he left was personal property worth no more than $100,000, you can use the **SMALL ESTATE AFFIDAVIT** as described on the next page.

THE SMALL ESTATE AFFIDAVIT

Suppose that the decedent had his affairs arranged so that the only thing in his name was a brokerage account worth $50,000 and coins in a safe deposit box worth $20,000. If the total value of all of the decedent's personal property is not greater than $100,000, the proper beneficiary can get possession of these items by giving the person who holds the property a **SMALL ESTATE AFFIDAVIT**. See Illinois statute (755 ILCS 5/25-1) for the statutory form of the Affidavit.

To use the Small Estate Affidavit all of the following must be true:

- ☑ The gross value of the decedent's personal property does not exceed $100,000.

- ☑ No Probate procedure is pending and none is necessary; in particular, there is no real property to be transferred by a Probate procedure in this or any other state.

- ☑ All of the decedent's funeral expenses have been paid or arrangements are made for their payment.

- ☑ There is no known claim against the decedent's estate.

If the decedent left a Will, you first need to file the Will with the Court and get a certified copy of that Will to attach to the Small Estate Affidavit. You will also need to attach a Certified copy of the death certificate to the Affidavit. See the end of Chapter 1, if you need to order copies of the death certificate.

COMPLETING THE AFFIDAVIT

You can get a copy of the Affidavit form by looking up the statute (755 ILCS 5/25-1).

IDENTITY OF AFFIANT

Whoever signs the Affidavit, i.e., the Affiant, should be the main beneficiary of the property to be transferred. If there are two adult children as sole beneficiaries, it is best they both sign the Affidavit. A beneficiary who lives out of state can transfer the property by Affidavit, provided he agrees to be bound by the laws of Illinois insofar as any transfer relating to the Affidavit.

IDENTITY OF BENEFICIARIES

See Chapter 5 for a discussion of who is to inherit the decedent's property. If there is any question in your mind, then it is best to consult with an attorney before attempting to take possession of the decedent's property.

THE SPOUSE AND CHILD AWARD

As explained on page 108, the decedent's surviving spouse and/or minor or dependent children are entitled to a minimum award of $10,000 plus $5,000 for each minor or dependent child. This award is free of creditor's claims.

TRANSFER TO MINOR

A Small Estate Affidavit can be used to transfer property to the parent or caretaker of a minor child without Court approval, provided the personal Estate of the child is no more than $10,000 (755 ILCS 5/25-2). Court approval is needed for transfers to a minor child that exceed $10,000. It is important to consult with an attorney when funds are left to a minor or dependent child.

IDENTITY OF CREDITORS

You need to identify all of the decedent's creditors (See Chapter 4). You need to make provision to pay any valid debt from the proceeds of the money you receive. If there are more debts than money, consult with an attorney before using this Affidavit.

CAUTION — PERSONAL LIABILITY

If you use the Affidavit, you become personally liable to anyone who had a right to the decedent's money. For example, if the decedent owed money on a credit card, and you neglected to pay that debt — or if some relative was entitled to receive a share of the money, and you did not give them their proper share. In such cases, the person who had a right to the property, can sue you personally for the amount of money you received using the Affidavit. If they win, you will need to return the money AND you will need to pay their attorney's fees (755 ILCS 5/25-1).

GETTING POSSESSION OF THE PROPERTY

You will need an Affidavit for each transfer of personal property. If the decedent left a valid Will, you will need to obtain a certified copy of the Will from the Clerk of the Probate Court and attach the copy to each Affidavit.

Once you have completed and properly signed the Affidavit, you may wish to call whoever has possession of the item (bank, stock broker, etc.) to make arrangements to have the property turned over to you. Before using the Affidavit, it is prudent to have an attorney review the document to verify that it is completed according to Illinois law.

USING THE SMALL ESTATE AFFIDAVIT TO TAKE CONTENTS OF SAFE DEPOSIT BOX

If the decedent leased a safe deposit box jointly with another, each with full authority to enter the box, the surviving lessee can enter the box and move all of its contents. If, however, the decedent and the co-lessee both needed to be present in order to access the box, or if the decedent was the sole lessee of a safe deposit box, a Personal Representative will need to be appointed who can take possession of the contents of the safe deposit box.

If a Personal Representative has not been appointed, you can take an inventory of the contents of the safe deposit box as explained at the end of Chapter 3. If you determine that Probate is not necessary, you may be able to transfer the contents of the box to the proper beneficiary by means of a Small Estate Affidavit.

If you are not the decedent's sole beneficiary, all of the adult beneficiaries identified the Small Estate Affidavit need to appoint you as their agent to take the contents of the box. They can do so by signing a document that says

> We appoint (name)_____ to act as our agent under the attached Small Estate Affidavit, to take possession of the contents of the decedent's safe deposit box (755 ILCS 5/25-1).

TRANSFERRING REAL PROPERTY

No Probate procedure is necessary to transfer real property if the decedent held that property as:
- ➪ the owner of a Life Estate - or -
- ➪ a Tenant By The Entirety - or -
- ➪ a Joint Tenant and Not as a Tenant In Common.

The survivor owner(s) owns the property as of the date of death, however, the decedent's name remains on the deed. Anyone examining title to the property will not know of the death. The Illinois Department of Public Health is responsible to issue the death certificate, but not to publish it or make it part of the public record. Of course, if there is a Probate proceeding, anyone can look up those public records and learn of the death.

If Probate is not necessary, it is a good idea to have an attorney prepare and record documents to notify anyone examining title to the property of the death. For Joint Tenants, the attorney can prepare a **DECEASED JOINT TENANT AFFIDAVIT**. The *Affidavit* is a sworn, written statement signed by the surviving joint owner. The Affidavit identifies the deceased owner. It gives the Permanent Real Estate Index Number, address and full legal description of the property. Once the Affidavit is recorded the decedent's name is, in effect, removed from the deed.

Probate is necessary if the decedent owned real property in his name only or jointly with another as Tenants-in-Common. The attorney for the Personal Representative will prepare and record a *Deed of Distribution* or alternatively a *Release of Estate's Interest in Real Estate*. If you are the beneficiary of that property, you should receive the original recorded Deed of Distribution or Release for your records.

> *Special Situation*

TRANSFERRING OUT OF STATE PROPERTY

Each state regulates the transfer of real property within that state. Many states, like Illinois, do not require that any document be recorded to transfer real property to a joint tenant who has a Right of Survivorship, or to a remainder beneficiary of a Life Estate interest. All the Grantee need do is keep a certified copy of the death certificate available to produce at closing when the property is transferred.

Some states allow the death certificate to be recorded in the county where the property is located, so that anyone examining title to the property will know who now owns the property. In other states, an Affidavit of Survivorship and proof of payment of Inheritance Taxes are recorded along with the death certificate. If the decedent owned out of state real property Jointly With Right of Survivorship, or if he owned a Life Estate interest, you may want to call the recording department in the county where the property is located to find out what documents (if any) need to be recorded to let people know that the surviving Grantee now owns the property. In Illinois, the County Recorder is in charge of recording deeds. In other states, it might be the Clerk of the Circuit Court, or the County Registrar.

Of course, if the decedent owned real property in his own name or as a Tenant In Common, you need to contact an attorney in that state to have the property transferred to the proper beneficiary.

SUMMARY ADMINISTRATION

Summary Administration is a shortened Probate procedure designed to help people obtain their inheritance quickly in cases where the Estate is small (not greater than $100,000) and there are no unusual circumstances, such as a Will contest or not enough money to pay all of the creditors.

Under Illinois law, Summary Administration is allowed, provided all of the following are true:

☑ The value of <u>all</u> of the property (both real and personal property) to be transferred in the state of Illinois does not exceed $100,000.

☑ There are no unpaid claims or all monies owed by the Estate are known to the beneficiaries of the Estate.

☑ There are no unpaid state or federal taxes, or provision has been made to pay the taxes.

☑ No one is entitled to a surviving spouse's or child's award, or if they are so entitled, the provision has been made for the minimum amount allowed by law.

☑ All beneficiaries have consented, in writing, to the distribution of the Estate by means of a Summary Administration (755 ILCS 5/9-8).

A petition must be filed asking the Probate Court to order the distribution of the assets to the proper beneficiaries. You can pick up the Petition for Summary Administration form in the office of the Clerk of the Probate Court. The Clerk is not authorized to assist you in completing the forms, nor to assist you in performing all of the necessary steps to obtain an Order of Summary Administration.

Although the Summary Administration procedure is relatively simple, it is best to consult with an attorney experienced in Probate matters to explain what needs to be done:

NOTICE TO CREDITORS
The court will set a hearing to determine if Summary Administration is appropriate. Prior to the hearing the person who files the petition must publish notice for three successive weeks in a newspaper of general circulation that is published in the county where the Probate is being conducted. The notice must give the decedent's date of death and tell when and where the hearing will be held.

OBTAIN BOND
To make sure that all of the decedent's bills are paid, the law requires that all of the beneficiaries be bonded. That means they must take out a bond equal to the amount each will receive. If it happens that a beneficiary must return his inheritance to pay any valid claim against the Estate, and he refuses, the bond can be used to make payment. But that doesn't mean that the beneficiary is off the hook. He can be personally sued by the bonding company to return the money, and if he loses, he will be required to pay his attorney's fees as well as the other person's attorney fees (755 ILCS 5/9-8).

ATTEND THE HEARING
It is best to have your attorney accompany you to the hearing. He knows what information the judge will require. If any problem turns up, your attorney will be able to assist you in solving that problem.

THE FULL PROBATE PROCEDURE

There needs to be a full Probate proceeding if the decedent left real property in his name only (or as a Tenant In Common) or personal property worth more than $100,000. The proceeding can take anywhere from several months to more than a year depending on the size and complexity of the Probate Estate. A Personal Representative must be appointed and Letters issued.

APPOINTING THE PERSONAL REPRESENTATIVE

The Court will appoint whoever is named as Personal Representative or Executor of the decedent's Will to serve. If that person is unable or unwilling to serve, the Court will appoint the Personal Representative using the order of priority as stated in Illinois statute 755 ILCS 5/9-3:

    1st the surviving spouse
    2nd the beneficiary of the decedent's Estate with preference given to his children
    3rd his children   4th his grandchildren
    5th his parents   6th his brothers and sisters
    7th his next of kin.

Anyone with priority can accept the appointment or they can appoint someone to be Personal Representative in their place.

If someone petitions the Court to be Personal Representative, and there is another with equal or greater priority, the petitioner must give the person with the same or greater priority at least 30 days notice that there will be a hearing on the matter. If those with the same or equal priority have no objection to the appointment, they can file a waiver of this notice (755 ILCS 5/9-5).

THE INDEPENDENT ADMINISTRATION

Illinois law is designed to speed administration and reduce costs by allowing the Personal Representative the right to act independently and without court supervision. This is called an *Independent Administration* (755 ILCS 5/28-1).

The Court will allow an Independent Administration unless the decedent's Will specifically requests that the Administration be supervised. But regardless of a request made in a Will, the judge will order a *Supervised Administration* if he finds that a beneficiary's interest will not be adequately protected, such as may be the case with a minor or disabled beneficiary (755 ILCS 5/28-2).

If the Court allows an Independent Administration, the *Independent Representative* can do all of the following without asking the Court for permission to do so:
- take possession of the Estate
- sell, lease or mortgage any of the Estate property
- borrow money on behalf of the decedent's Estate
- continue the decedent's business
- settle claims against the decedent's Estate
- employ agents, accountants, attorneys
- invest money of the Estate

(755 ILCS 5/28-8).

The Independent Representative may make the Spouse and Child's Award as described in Chapter 4, without Court approval. He will need to seek Court approval if the amount he wishes to transfer exceeds 5% of the gross value of the Estate as of the date of death — unless the amount to be transferred is not greater than the minimum amount as allowed by Illinois law (755 ILCS 5/28-7).

YOUR RIGHTS AS A BENEFICIARY

The Personal Representative is in charge of settling the Estate. Too often, beneficiaries of the Estate have no idea of what is going on. They wait to receive their inheritance, not knowing that they have rights under Illinois law; and more importantly, not knowing how to assert their rights.

❖ RIGHT TO BE KEPT INFORMED

Anyone who has an interest in the Estate has the right to be kept informed beginning with notice of who is being appointed as Personal Representative. If there is a valid Will, the person named as Executor will be appointed. If the decedent died without a Will, whoever is appointed must, within 14 days, send you written notice of his appointment — unless you sign a waiver of such notice (755 ILCS 5/9-5).

❖ RIGHT TO OBJECT TO PERSONAL REPRESENTATIVE

Regardless of who has priority to serve, it is the Court who has final say as to who will serve as Personal Representative. The judge can appoint the person with priority, or if the beneficiaries of the Estate object, he can appoint someone else. You can raise any objection you may have to the Court; however, unless the Personal Representative:
- ☒ is not yet 18 years old, or
- ☒ is not a resident of the United States, or
- ☒ is not of sound mind; i.e., is disabled as determined by the Court, or
- ☒ has been convicted of a felony (755 ILCS 5/6-13)

it may be difficult to convince the Court that the Personal Representative is not qualified to serve.

Before bringing your concerns before the Court it is important to consult with your own attorney.

❖ RIGHT TO YOUR OWN ATTORNEY

The attorney who handles the Estate is employed by, and represents, the Personal Representative. If the Estate is sizeable, then you might consider employing your own attorney to check that things are done properly and in a timely manner. Even if the Estate is small, consider consulting with an attorney any time you are concerned about the way the Probate is being conducted.

❖ RIGHT TO A HEARING BEFORE THE COURT

If an Independent Administration is being conducted, you have the right, at any time, to petition (ask) the Court to conduct a hearing on any matter that is troubling you (755 ILCS 5/28-5). If a Supervised Administration is being conducted, you still have a right to go before the Court if you believe something is seriously wrong, however, you may want to consult with an experienced Probate attorney. He can explain the best way for you to present your concerns to the Court. He can tell you what arguments have a good chance of swaying the judge. And he can tell you which arguments have so little probability of success that they are not worth pursuing.

❖ RIGHT TO OBJECT TO THE WILL

The decedent's Will can be admitted into Probate upon the testimony or Affidavit of at least two witnesses to the Will (755 ILCS 5/6-4). You have the right to receive a copy of the Will that is offered for Probate. If you believe the Will is not valid, you can bring your concerns to the attention of the Court, but this is one of those issues that requires the assistance of an experienced Probate attorney. The person who offers the Will into Probate is not about to withdraw that Will without a fight. That fight is called litigation — with the validity of the Will being decided at trial.

✧ RIGHT TO DEMAND A SUPERVISED ADMINISTRATION

If the Court allows an Independent Administration, the Personal Representative is required to send notice to each beneficiary that he is appointed to act independently, and to give the beneficiary a form that can be used to object to the Independent Administration (755 ILCS 5/28-2).

Allowing the Personal Representative to act independently can save the Estate money, but the downside is that without Court supervision the Representative can do some serious mischief. Do not hesitate to fill out the form and mail it to the Court if you have serious concerns about the ability of the Representative to properly administer the Estate. The Court will either grant your request for a Supervised Administration or will hold a hearing on the matter and then rule on your request.

✧ RIGHT TO DEMAND BOND

It doesn't happen often, but every now and again a Personal Representative will run off with Estate funds. A bond is insurance for the Estate. If Estate monies are stolen, the company that issued the bond will reimburse the Estate for the loss. It is up to the Court to decide whether a bond or other security is necessary. In general, the Court will order bond if the Personal Representative is not a resident of Illinois. The Court will not order a bond if the Personal Representative is an authorized bank or trust company.

The Court may decide not to require bond if the Personal Representative is excused by Will from giving bond or security; but to protect the Estate assets, the Court may require Estate funds to be deposited with a bank or broker subject to the further order of the Court (755 ILCS 5/12-1, 5/12-4, 755 ILCS 5/6-13).

Most Wills state that no bond shall be required. The reason is two-fold. The Will maker chooses someone he trusts to administer the Estate, so he does not think a bond is necessary. And there are economic reasons. The cost of the bond is paid for by the Estate, and ultimately the amount inherited is reduced by the amount paid for the bond.

If the decedent died without a Will, or if the Will makes no mention of security, you (the beneficiary) may be asked to file a request with the Court to waive bond. The cost of the bond should not be a factor if there is any danger of the Estate property belong lost or mismanaged. If you are concerned about the safety of the Estate assets, it is important that you not sign a waiver, but rather ask the Court to order the Personal Representative to be bonded.

✧ RIGHT TO KNOW PERSONAL REPRESENTATIVE'S FEES

The Personal Representative is entitled to be compensated for his efforts in settling the Estate. If he is also a beneficiary of the Estate he may decide not to take a commission and just take his inheritance. The reason may be economic. Any fee the Representative takes is taxable as ordinary income, but monies inherited are not taxable to him as a beneficiary. Ask the Personal Representative to tell you, in writing, whether he intends to charge a fee, and if so, how much.

Although Illinois statute (755 ILCS 5/27-1) states that the Personal Representative is entitled to reasonable compensation, there are no statutory guidelines for what is "reasonable." If you think the amount charged is unreasonable, you can ask the Court to set a hearing on the matter. But before doing so, you should consult with an experienced Probate attorney to determine whether the amount being charged is the "going rate."

✧ RIGHT TO KNOW THE ATTORNEY'S FEES

The job of administering the decedent's Estate is complex and there is potential liability associated with it. The Personal Representative must settle the Estate by paying all valid claims, taxes and costs of Administration. Monies are paid from the decedent's Estate and not from the Personal Representative's pocket. However, if he makes a mistake, he may be responsible to pay for it (755 ILCS 5/24-18). For example, if the Personal Representative pays a debt that did not need to be paid, or if he transfers property to the beneficiaries too quickly and there were outstanding taxes, he may be responsible to pay for his error.

The Personal Representative has the right to employ an attorney to guide him through the Probate procedure so that things will be done properly and at no personal cost to the Representative. It is proper to have the attorney paid with Estate funds (755 ILCS 5/27-2). You, as a beneficiary of the Estate, have the right to know how much will be charged for legal fees. Ask the Personal Representative to give you a copy of the retainer agreement. If the attorney is employed on an hourly basis, have the attorney give a written estimate of the time he expects to spend on the Probate proceeding.

There is no statutory guideline for what is a "reasonable" fee for the attorney. You could call different law firms and ask what they charge to Probate an Estate with similar assets and that will give you some idea of the going rate. If after doing some "comparison shopping" you believe that the attorney's fee is not reasonable, you can negotiate with him to lower the fee. If you cannot reach an agreement, you can ask the Probate Court to set a hearing to settle the matter.

✦ RIGHT TO COPY OF INVENTORY

If the Probate is being conducted with Court supervision, the Personal Representative must file an inventory of all of the assets of the Probate Estate within sixty days of his appointment. You can request that he give you a copy of the inventory as soon as it is filed with the Court (755 ILCS 5/14-1).

The Personal Representative does not need to file an inventory with the Court if there is an Independent Administration, but if he is bonded, he is required to give the company that issued the bond (the *surety*) a copy of the inventory within 90 days. If you give the Representative a written request for a copy of the inventory, he must give you a copy as well (755 ILCS 5/28-6).

The value of the inventory is used to determine the Representative's fees and to determine how much taxes need to be paid. It is important that you receive a copy of the inventory, and that you are satisfied with the value assigned to each item.

✦ RIGHT TO AN APPRAISAL

The Personal Representative may employ an appraiser to assist in determining the value of items included in the Estate inventory — but he is not required to have a formal appraisal unless ordered by the Court (755 ILCS 5/14-2). If you do not agree with the value assigned to any Probate asset, you have the right to ask the Personal Representative to have the item appraised. If he refuses, you can ask Court to order an independent appraisal of the item

❖ RIGHT TO AN ACCOUNTING

Before closing the Estate, the Personal Representative of a Supervised Administration must file an accounting with the Court, starting with the inventory value of the Estate and ending with the amount to be distributed to the beneficiaries (755 ILCS 5/24-1).

In an Independent Administration, the accounting does not need to be filed with the Court, but the Personal Representative is required to furnish a copy to you (755 ILCS 5/28-11(a) and (b)). If the Estate has significant assets, you may want your own accountant to look over the accounting. If there are any problems that your accountant cannot resolve with the Personal Representative, you can raise these issues at the hearing.

You may be asked to sign a waiver of your right to an accounting, but keep in mind that the accounting is for your benefit. There are few situations that justify giving up your right to know how Estate monies were spent.

❖ RIGHT TO HAVE THE ESTATE CLOSED WITHOUT DELAY

How long it takes to complete the Probate proceeding depends on the size and complexity of the matter. As explained in Chapter 4, the Personal Representative must give creditors an opportunity to come forward and present their claims. Creditors have six months from the first day that notice was published or three months from the date he was given notice by mail, whichever is the later date. If there are no outstanding debts, the Estate may be closed at the end of these time periods.

If an Estate Tax Return is filed, it will probably take more than a year before tax clearance is received and the Personal Representative can close out the Estate. The beneficiaries are entitled to an annual accounting if it takes more than a year to settle the Estate (755 ILCS 5/24-1)

If you do not receive an accounting and a proposed plan of distribution within these time periods, you have the right to ask the Court to order the Personal Representative to settle the Estate (755 ILCS 5/24-16).

✧ RIGHT TO RECEIVE A DEBT FREE INHERITANCE

Once a beneficiary finally receives his inheritance, about the last thing he wants to hear is that there is some unfinished business, or worse yet that monies need to be paid from the inheritance he received. But that is just what could happen if the Personal Representative fails to file a return, or fails to pay taxes, or if he under-reports a tax obligation. You should ask to see a copy of all of the tax returns that were filed, and then verify that any monies that were due have been paid. Most importantly, you should not agree to having the Estate closed if the closing statement shows that there are any outstanding debts that need to be paid.

IT'S YOUR RIGHT - DON'T BE INTIMIDATED

You may feel uncomfortable being assertive with a friend or family member who is Personal Representative. Don't be. It's your money and your right to be informed. Be especially firm if the Personal Representative waves you off with "You've known me for years. Surely you trust me." People who are trustworthy, don't ask to be trusted. They do what is right. The very fact that the Personal Representative is resisting is a red flag. In such situation, you can explain that it is not a matter of trust, but a matter of what is your legal right.

At the same time, keep things in perspective. Your relationship with the Personal Representative may be more important to you than the money you inherit. The job of settling an Estate can be complex and demanding. If the Personal Representative is getting the job done, let him know you appreciate his efforts.

THE CHECK LIST

We discussed many things that need to be done when someone dies in the state of Illinois. The next page contains a check list that you may find helpful.

You can check those items that you need to do, and then cross them off the list once they are done. We made the list as comprehensive as possible, so many items may not apply in your case. In such case, you can cross them off the list or mark them *N/A* (not applicable).

Things To Do

FUNERAL ARRANGEMENTS TO BE MADE
- ☐ AUTOPSY   ☐ ANATOMICAL GIFT
- ☐ DISPOSITION OF BODY OR ASHES

DEATH CERTIFICATE
GIVE COPY TO: _____
_____
_____

NOTICE OF DEATH
PEOPLE TO BE NOTIFIED _____

COMPANIES TO NOTIFY
- ☐ TELEPHONE COMPANY
  - ☐ LOCAL CARRIER   ☐ LONG DISTANCE   ☐ CELLULAR
- ☐ NEWSPAPER (OBITUARY PRINTED)
- ☐ NEWSPAPER DELIVERY CANCELLED   ☐ deposit refund
- ☐ SOCIAL SECURITY
- ☐ INTERNET SERVER CANCELLED
- ☐ TELEVISION CABLE/SATELLITE COMPANY CANCELLED
- ☐ POWER & LIGHT   ☐ deposit refund
- ☐ POST OFFICE
- ☐ OTHER UTILITIES (GAS, WATER)   ☐ deposit refund
- ☐ PENSION PLAN
- ☐ ANNUITY
- ☐ HEALTH INSURANCE COMPANY
- ☐ LIFE INSURANCE COMPANY
- ☐ HOME INSURANCE COMPANY
- ☐ MOTOR VEHICLE INSURANCE COMPANY
- ☐ CONDOMINIUM OR HOMEOWNER ASSOCIATION
- ☐ CANCEL SERVICE CONTRACT   ☐ deposit refund
- ☐ CREDIT CARD COMPANIES

_____
_____
_____

Things To Do

REMOVE DECEDENT AS BENEFICIARY OF:
- ☐ WILL   ☐ INSURANCE POLICY   ☐ PENSION PLAN
- ☐ BANK OR IRA ACCOUNT   ☐ SECURITY

DEBTS
PAY DECEDENT'S DEBTS (AMOUNT & CREDITOR)
_____

COLLECT MONIES OWED TO DECEDENT (AMOUNT & DEBTOR)
_____

TAXES
- ☐ FILE FINAL FEDERAL INCOME TAX RETURN
- ☐ FILE FINAL STATE INCOME TAX RETURN
- ☐ RECEIVE INCOME TAX REFUND
- ☐ FILE ESTATE TAX RETURN

PROPERTY TO BE TRANSFERRED
- ☐ PERSONAL EFFECTS
- ☐ MOTOR VEHICLE
- ☐ BANK ACCOUNT
- ☐ CREDIT UNION ACCOUNT
- ☐ IRA ACCOUNT
- ☐ SECURITIES
- ☐ BROKERAGE ACCOUNT
- ☐ INSURANCE PROCEEDS
- ☐ HOMESTEAD
- ☐ TIME SHARE
- ☐ OTHER REAL PROPERTY
- ☐ CONTENTS OF SAFE DEPOSIT BOX

OTHER THINGS TO DO
_____
_____
_____

WHAT TO KEEP — WHAT TO THROW AWAY

Once the Probate proceeding is over, you will be left with many documents and wonder which you need to keep:

COURT DOCUMENTS

You should keep a copy of the inventory to establish the value of property that you inherit. That value becomes your basis for any Capital Gains Tax that you may need to pay in the future. Other than the inventory, there is no reason to keep any Court document, provided you are satisfied with the way things were done; and do not intend to take action against the Personal Representative, or his attorney. The Clerk of the Probate Court keeps the Probate file on record, so if for some reason you later need a copy of a Probate document, you can get it from the Clerk.

PERSONAL RECORDS

The surviving spouse, or if no spouse, his next of kin should keep the decedent's personal papers (birth certificate, marriage certificate, naturalization papers, army records, religious documents, etc.). They may be needed in order to apply for government, or other, benefits. The next of kin may want to keep the decedent's medical records in the event that a family member needs to check out a genetic disorder.

TAX RECORDS

The IRS has up to three years to collect additional taxes, and you have up to seven years to claim a loss from a worthless security, so you should keep the decedent's tax file for seven years from the date of filing the return. You can learn more about which records to keep from the IRS publication 552. You can get the publication by calling the IRS at (800) 829-3676 or you can download it from their Web site: http://www.irs.gov

Everyman's Estate Plan 7

The first six chapters of this book describe how to wind up the affairs of the decedent. As you read those chapters, you learned about the kinds of problems that can occur when settling the decedent's Estate. It is relatively simple for you to set up an Estate Plan so that your family members are not burdened with similar problems. An *Estate Plan* is the arranging of your finances for maximum control and protection during your lifetime, and at the same time ensuring that your property will be transferred quickly and at little cost to your heirs.

If you think that only wealthy people need to prepare an Estate Plan, you are mistaken. Each year, beneficiaries of relatively modest Estates, spend thousands of dollars to settle an Estate. A bit of planning could have eliminated most, if not all, of the expense and hassle suffered by those families.

The suggestions in this chapter are designed to assist the average person in preparing a practical and inexpensive Estate Plan, so we named this chapter EVERYMAN'S ESTATE PLAN.

Once you create your own Estate Plan, you can be assured that your family will not be left with more problems than happy memories of you.

AVOIDING PROBATE

After reading the last Chapter, many will come to the conclusion that Probate is a good thing to avoid. Those who have $100,000 or less may not be concerned with avoiding Probate because, as explained in the last Chapter, your beneficiaries can get possession of that property with little effort or expense by using a Small Estate Affidavit or a Summary Administration procedure.

But if you own property in excess of $100,000 in your name only, a full Probate will be necessary with all of its inherent delays and expenses. Notice that the operative phrase in the last sentence is *in your name only*. Whether a Probate procedure is necessary depends on how your property is titled (owned). It makes no difference whether you do or do not have a Will. If you own more than $100,000, and that property is titled in your name only, your beneficiaries will need to go through a Probate procedure in order to get possession of that property.

As explained in Chapter 5, there are many ways to title real property so that it passes automatically without the need for Probate. For example, if you own real property Jointly with Rights of Survivorship, upon your death the survivors will own the property without the need to go through Probate. Similarly if you own a Life Estate interest, upon your death the property passes directly to the owner of the remainder interest in the property.

In this Chapter we will examine ways to title your personal property (bank accounts, securities, etc.) so that it passes to your beneficiaries without the need for Probate.

OWNERSHIP OF BANK ACCOUNTS

You can arrange to have all of your bank accounts set up so that should you die, the money goes directly to a beneficiary. For example, suppose all you own is a bank account and you want whatever you have in the account to go to your son and daughter when you die. You might think that a simple solution is to put each child's name on the account as joint tenants with Right of Survivorship, but first consider the problems associated with a joint account.

⊠ POTENTIAL LIABILITY

If you hold a bank account jointly with your adult child and that child is sued or gets a divorce, the child may need to disclose his ownership of the joint account. In such a case, you may find yourself spending money to prove that the account was established for your convenience only and that all of the money in that account really belongs to you.

⊠ OVERREACHING

If you set up a joint account with your child so that the child has authority to withdraw funds from the account, monies could be withdrawn without your knowledge or consent.

If you open a multiple party account with two of your children, there is the problem of what happens to the funds after your death. Should you die, your share of the account belongs to the surviving joint owners, equally (765 ILCS 1005/2(a)). But as a practical matter each joint owner has free access to the joint account. After your death the first child to the bank may decide to withdraw all of the money and that will, at the very least, cause hard feelings between them.

THE BENEFICIARY ACCOUNT

Holding a bank account jointly with a family member eliminates the need for Probate, but at the cost of control of the funds. One way to avoid Probate of the account yet retain full control during your lifetime, is to name one or more persons to be the beneficiary of the account. There are two forms of ***Beneficiary Account***. When you open your account you can direct the bank to hold your account ***In Trust For*** ("ITF") one or more beneficiaries that you name; or you can have a contract with the bank that directs the bank to ***Pay On Death*** ("POD") all of the money in the account to one or more beneficiaries.

The contract you sign with the bank gives instructions that the bank will follow should you die while the account is open. If you open an In Trust For or Pay On Death account, unless the contract with your bank states differently, under Illinois law:

⇨ The beneficiary does not have any right to the account during your lifetime.

⇨ you are free to change beneficiaries without asking the beneficiary's permission to do so.

⇨ you can add to or withdraw money from the account without the knowledge or consent of the beneficiary

⇨ If you name two or more beneficiaries, upon your death, the funds are divided equally between them as Tenants In Common, i.e., without rights of survivorship
(205 ILCS 625/3, 625/4).

TRANSFER ON DEATH SECURITIES

The Illinois law for securities is much the same as the statutes for bank accounts. You can arrange to have a security (a stock, bond or brokerage account) transferred to a beneficiary upon your death. You can instruct the holder of the security to Pay On Death ("POD") or **Transfer On Death** ("TOD") to a named beneficiary.

If the beneficiary of the security dies before you, the security will become part of your Estate. However, you can direct that if the beneficiary dies first, his descendants inherit the security. For example, a security account can be titled as: Alice Lee TOD Wayne Lee LDPS, which is shorthand for:

> Alice Lee is the owner of the securities account. On her death, transfer the securities in her account to Wayne Lee. If Wayne dies before Alice, give the securities to Wayne's lineal descendants, per stirpes.

The is much the same as the POD account. Wayne has no right to the securities until Alice dies. Alice is free to close the account or to change the beneficiary of the security without permission from Wayne (815 ILCS 10/5, 10/7, 10/10).

There may be times when you wish to hold a security account jointly (say with your spouse) and have your children inherit the security when you both die.

For example:
> ELDON CONNORS LORRAINE CONNORS, JT TEN
> TOD FRED CONNORS and MARIE CONNORS

⇨ Fred and Marie have no right to the account during the lifetime of their parents.

⇨ Should either parent die, the surviving spouse owns the account, and is free to close the account or change the beneficiary of the account.

⇨ Once both parents are deceased, Fred and Marie will inherit the security with each owning an equal share.

⇨ Should either child die before his parent, then unless the account is changed, the surviving beneficiary will inherit the account.

⇨ Should both children die before their parents, the security will belong to the Estate of the last parent to die (815 ILCS 10/2, 10/5, 10/6, 10/7)

If your Estate consists only of bank accounts and/or securities, and you want all of your property to go to one or two beneficiaries without the need for Probate, but with maximum control and protection of your funds during your lifetime, then holding your property in any of these beneficiary forms:

In Trust For
Pay On Death
Transfer On Death

should accomplish your goal.

GIFT TO A MINOR CHILD

At the beginning of this chapter, we identified two problems with a joint account: potential liability if the joint owner is sued and overreaching by the joint owner. If you wish to make a gift to a minor child, that presents still another problem. The Beneficiary Account (POD or ITF) avoids the problem of potential liability and overreaching, but if the beneficiary of your account is a minor, there is the problem of the child having access to a large sum of money.

Under Illinois law, if the amount in the account is under $50,000 the financial institution may transfer the funds to a trust company or to an adult member of the minor's family. Court authority is necessary if the amount to be transferred exceeds that amount (760 ILCS 20/8). The Court may decide to appoint a Guardian to care for the child's property. Even if the amount to be transferred is less than $50,000, the financial institution might refuse to transfer the funds without authorization from the Court.

You may think it best that the child inherits more than $50,000, this way a Court will see to it that the monies are held safely till the child is an adult. But that only presents a new set of problems. It takes time, effort and money to set up a Guardianship. If you leave the child a significant amount of money, then the Guardian has the right to be paid to manage those funds. It could happen that the cost of the Guardianship significantly reduces the amount of money inherited by the child. There are ways to avoid the problem of having a Guardian appointed to care for property inherited by a child, and yet ensuring that the monies are protected. One such method is the ILLINOIS UNIFORM TRANSFERS TO MINORS ACT.

THE UNIFORM TRANSFERS TO MINORS ACT

The *Illinois Uniform Transfers to Minors Ac*t is designed to protect gifts made to a minor by appointing someone to be the *Custodian* of a gift until the child is an adult. For example, you can make a minor child the beneficiary of your life insurance policy and name a trusted relative or friend to be the Custodian of the gift. Should you die while the child is a minor, the insurance company will give the proceeds of the policy to the person you named as Custodian to hold until the child is an adult.

You can make a gift to a minor in your Will. You can appoint your Personal Representative (or anyone else) as Custodian of the gift. For example:
    I give the sum of $20,000 to_____ (name) as custodian for _____ (name of minor) under the Illinois Uniform Transfers to Minors Act.

THE LIFETIME GIFT
You can even use the Illinois Uniform Transfers to Minors Law to make gifts during your lifetime of items such as shares in a corporation or a limited partnership interest. You can nominate yourself as Custodian of the gift, or you can name another person to serve as Custodian. Once the lifetime gift is made it becomes irrevocable, so this method is not appropriate unless you are sure that you want the child to have the gift once he/she is an adult.

In general, the Custodian must distribute the gift when the child reaches 18; however, if you make a lifetime gift, or a gift as part of your Will, the Custodian is not required to distribute the gift until the child reaches 21 (760 ILCS 20/4, 20/5, 20/10, 20/21).

The Custodian needs to invest and manage the property in a responsible, prudent manner. He must keep records of all transactions made with custodial property; and make those records available for inspection by the child's parent, or legal representative, or the child, if the minor is 14 or older. If those records are not to their satisfaction, they can petition (ask) the Probate Court to require the Custodian to give an accounting (760 ILCS 20/13, 20/20).

The Custodian has the discretion to use the gift to care for the child. The Custodian can pay monies directly to the child, or can use the money for the child's benefit. The Custodian can refuse to use any of the monies for the child and just keep the funds invested until it is time to distribute the funds. If the Custodian wants to keep the funds invested, the child's parent, or his legal representative, or the child once he is 14, can ask the Judge of the Probate Court to order the Custodian to part with some or all of the money for the benefit of the child. The Judge will decide what is in the child's best interest and then rule on the matter (760 ILCS 20/15).

The Custodian is entitled to be paid for his effort each year (760 ILCS 20/16). If the gift is sizeable, the Custodian's fee can be sizeable. Before appointing a person or a financial institution as Custodian, it is best to come to a written agreement about what will be charged to manage the custodial property.

A gift made under the Illinois Uniform Transfers to Minors Act is limited to one minor only (760 ILCS 20/11). If you want to give a single gift, such as a gift of real property to two or more children or if you want more flexibility about when the minor is to receive the gift, then a Trust may be the better way to go. We will discuss Trusts later in this chapter.

THE GIFT OF REAL PROPERTY

As explained in Chapter 5, if you own real property together with another, then who owns the property upon your death depends on how the Grantee is identified on the face of the deed. If you compare the Grantee clause of the deed to the examples given in Chapter 5 you can determine who will inherit the property when you die. If you are not satisfied with the way the property will be inherited, you need to consult with an attorney to change the deed so that it will conform to your wishes.

If you own the property in your name only or as a Tenant In Common, when you die, there will need to be a Probate proceeding to determine the proper beneficiary of that land. If your main objective is to avoid Probate, you can have an attorney change the deed so that upon your death, the property will descend to your beneficiary without the need for Probate. As with bank and securities accounts there are different ways to do so, each with its own advantages and disadvantages.

JOINT OWNERSHIP

If you hold property in your name only, and wish to avoid Probate, you can have your deed changed so that you and a beneficiary are joint owners with rights of survivorship. If you do so, should either of you die, the other will own the property 100%. That avoids Probate, but by making that person joint owner, you are, in effect, making a gift of half of the property during your lifetime. You will not be able to sell that property without the beneficiary's permission. And if the beneficiary gives permission and the property is sold, the beneficiary will have the legal right to half of the proceeds of the sale. As explained on the next page, you may be creating tax problems as well.

You can arrange to sell your home without paying a Capital Gains Tax (see page 42), but if you make someone joint owner of your home who does not live with you, a Capital Gains Tax may need to be paid on the joint owner's share of the proceeds should you decide to sell the property.

CAUTION — GIFT OF HOMESTEAD

Some elderly parents worry that they may need nursing care at some time in the future and lose all of their life savings to pay for that care. The parent may decide that the best way to avoid Probate and protect the homestead from loss is to transfer the homestead to their child with the understanding that the parent will continue to live there until he/she dies. But this is just trading risks.

⊠ RISK OF LOSS

Property transferred to your child could be lost if the child runs into serious financial difficulties or gets sued. This is especially a risk if your child is a professional (doctor, nurse, accountant, financial planner, attorney, etc.). If your child is (or gets) married, then this complicates matters even more so. If the child is divorced, the property may need to be included as part of the settlement agreement. This may be to your child's detriment because the child may need to share the value of the property with his/her former spouse. If you do not transfer the property, it cannot become part of the marital equation.

☒ LOSS OF HOMESTEAD TAX CREDIT

As explained in Chapter 2, those filing an Illinois income tax return are entitled to a 5% tax credit of real property taxes paid on their principal residence (35 ILCS 5/208). In addition, Homeowners' Tax Exemptions are allowed for any number of reasons such as the owner being aged, a disabled veteran, or the surviving spouse of a blind person or of a disabled veteran (35 ILCS 200/15-170, 200/15/175).

If you transfer your homestead, you will lose your right to receive these tax breaks.

☒ LOSS OF HOMESTEAD CREDITOR PROTECTION

Up to $15,000 ($30,000 if owned jointly) of the value of your homestead is protected from creditors during your lifetime. This may not seem like much, but it could keep a roof over your head if the equity in your home is under that value. For example, suppose you and your spouse own a home worth $200,000 with a mortgage of $190,000. With few exceptions, such as property taxes and the mortgage on your home, none of your creditors can force the sale of your property (735 ILCS 5/12-901).

By transferring your home to a child, you lose your homestead protection against creditors. If the child does not occupy that property as his homestead, there is no homestead creditor protection whatsoever. The child's creditors can force the sale of the property (that's your home) for relatively small amounts of unpaid debts.

☒ POSSIBLE GIFT TAX

If the value of the transfer is worth more than $11,000 you need to file a Gift Tax return. For most of us, this is not a problem because no Gift Tax need be paid unless the value of the property (plus the value of all gifts in excess of the Annual Gift Tax Exclusion that you gave over your lifetime) exceeds $1,000,000 (see Page 40). But if your Estate is in that tax bracket, you need to be aware that you are "using up" your lifetime Gift Tax Exclusion.

☒ POSSIBLE CAPITAL GAINS TAX

Although Congress has expressed an intent to phase out the Estate Tax, there is no discussion to do away with the Capital Gains Tax. If you gift the property to the child during your lifetime, when he sells the property, he will pay a Capital Gains Tax on the increase in value from the price you paid for your home to the selling price at the time your child sells the property.

If you do not make the gift during your lifetime, the child will inherit the property with a step-up in basis, i.e., he will inherit the property at its market value as of your date of death. Under today's tax structure and continuing until 2009, that step-up in basis is unlimited. If your child sells the property shortly after he inherits it, he will pay no Capital Gains Tax, regardless of how large the step-up in basis.

In 2010, there will be a limit on the amount that can be inherited free of the Capital Gains Tax; but that limit is quite high, so for most of us this is not a concern.

☒ POSSIBLE LOSS OF GOVERNMENT BENEFITS

If you transfer property, then depending upon the value of the transfer, you could be disqualified from receiving Medicaid or Supplemental Security Income ("SSI") benefits for a substantial period of time. When a person applies for Medicaid, he must disclose if, within three years of his application, he transferred property for less than its fair market value (i.e. he gifted property).

This reporting period extends to five years if the transfer was to a Trust. The Medicaid agency will compute a disqualification period depending on the value of the transfer. This can present a serious problem should you need extended nursing care during that period of time.

Under current state and federal law, there are many ways to protect your homestead and still qualify for government benefits. Before transferring your homestead because of your concern for the cost of future health care, consult with an Elder Law attorney. He will be able to suggest ways to protect your assets, and still ensure that you receive the health care that you may require in your later years.

THE LIFE ESTATE, NOT A COMPLETE SOLUTION

Some of the problems we have discussed regarding an outright gift of the homestead, can be avoided by transferring home and keeping a Life Estate for yourself. This means that you have the right to occupy the property for as long as you live. Once you die your beneficiary will own the property without any need for Probate, but again there are downsides:

- You cannot sell the property during your lifetime without the beneficiary agreeing to the sale.

- If you sell the property, the beneficiary is entitled to some portion of the proceeds of the sale.

- If you or your beneficiary become incapacitated, the property cannot be sold unless a Guardian is appointed.

Before making any transfer of real property, it is important to consult with an Elder Law attorney and/or certified financial planner and/or accountant to examine all aspects related to the transfer.

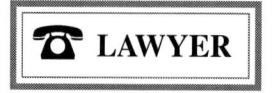

| ☎ LAWYER | OUT OF STATE PROPERTY |

Each state is in charge of the way property located in that state is transferred. If you own property in another state (or country), you need to consult with a local attorney to determine how that property will be transferred to your beneficiaries once you die. Many state laws are similar to Illinois, namely, property held as **JOINT TENANTS WITH RIGHT OF SURVIVORSHIP** or a **LIFE ESTATE INTEREST** are transferred without the need for Probate.

If you own property in another state in your name only, or as a **TENANT IN COMMON,** or if you own property with your spouse in a Community Property state, a Probate procedure may need to be conducted in that state. If it is necessary to have a Probate proceeding in Illinois, then a second (*ancillary*) Probate proceeding may need to be conducted in the state where the property is located. This could have the effect of doubling the cost of Probate.

Still another problem is the matter of taxes. Inheritance taxes may be due in the state where the property is located. It may be necessary to file an income tax and/or an Estate Tax return in two states. In addition to increased taxes, this can double the cost of the accounting fees.

You may wish to consult with an attorney for suggestions about how to set up your Estate Plan to avoid such problems.

A TRUST MAY BE THE SOLUTION (OR NOT)

A full Probate procedure may be necessary if you hold property in your name only or as a Tenant In Common. We explored different ways to re-title property to avoid Probate, but these methods have trade-offs that may be unacceptable to you. One way to avoid many of these potential problems is to set up a **Revocable Living Trust** (also known as an *Inter Vivos Trust*).

A Revocable Living Trust is designed to care for your property during your lifetime, and then to distribute your property once you die — without the need for Probate. You may have been encouraged to set up a Trust by your financial planner, attorney, or accountant. Even people of modest means are being encouraged to use a Trust as the basis of their Estate Plan. But Trusts have their pros and cons. Before getting into that, let's first discuss what a Trust is and how it works:

SETTING UP A TRUST

To create a Trust, a person has his attorney prepare a Trust document (a *Trust Agreement*) in accordance with his (the client's) needs and desires. The Agreement is between the person who creates and funds the Trust (the **Settlor** or *Grantor*) and the **Trustee** (manager) of property placed in the Trust. The Settlor usually appoints himself as Trustee so that he is in total control of property he places into the Trust. This means that he signs the Trust Agreement as the Settlor and also as the Trustee who promises to manage the property according to the terms of the Trust Agreement. The Trust document also names a **Successor Trustee** who will take over the management of the Trust property should the Trustee resign, become disabled, or die. We will refer to the Revocable Living Trust as the "Living Trust" or just the "Trust" and the person who creates the Trust as the "Settlor."

Once the Trust Agreement is properly signed, the Settlor transfers property into the Trust. He does this by changing title from his individual name to his name as Trustee. For example, if Elaine Richards sets up a Trust naming herself as Trustee, and she wishes to place her bank account into the Trust, all she need do is instruct the bank to change the name on the account from Elaine Richards to:

> ELAINE RICHARDS, TRUSTEE OF THE ELAINE RICHARDS REVOCABLE TRUST AGREEMENT DATED JULY 12, 2004.

When the change is made, all the money in the account becomes Trust property. Elaine (wearing her Trustee hat) has total control of the account, taking money out, and putting money in, as she sees fit. Similarly, if she wants to put real property into the Trust, she can have her attorney prepare a new deed with the owner identified as ELAINE RICHARDS, TRUSTEE. See Chapter 5 for an example of real property placed into a Trust.

Because the Trust is revocable, if she wishes, Elaine can terminate the Trust and have all the Trust property returned and placed back into her own individual name. If she does not revoke the Trust during her lifetime, once she dies the Trust becomes irrevocable, and her Successor Trustee must follow the terms of the Trust Agreement as written. If the Trust says to give the Trust property to certain beneficiaries, the Successor Trustee will do so, and without the need for Probate. If the Trust directs the Successor Trustee to continue to hold property in Trust and use the money to take care of a member of Elaine's family, then the Successor Trustee will do so.

Setting up a Trust has many good features.

✩✩ AVOID PROBATE

Probate can be time consuming and very expensive. Both the Personal Representative and his attorney are entitled to payment for their services. These fees can be significant. It may be necessary to employ accountants and appraisers, and real estate brokers to sell property as well. If you have property in two states, then two Probate procedures may be necessary (one in each state) and that could be costly in time, effort and money. If the Trust is properly drafted and your property placed into the Trust, you should be able to avoid Probate altogether.

✩ FEDERAL ESTATE TAX SAVINGS

Many people think that the federal Estate Tax will be phased out so that by 2010, no Estate Taxes will be due regardless of the size of an Estate. But under current law, federal Estate Taxes are scheduled to be reinstated in 2011. As explained in Chapter 2, Estates that exceed $1,000,000 will be subject to both state and federal Estates Taxes.

A couple with an Estate in excess of a million dollars can reduce the risk of an Estate Tax by setting up a Trust, so that each partner can take advantage of his own Estate Tax Exclusion. For example, suppose a couple owns two million dollars. They can set up a single Trust that separates the money into two Trusts once one partner dies. The Trust can be arranged so that the surviving spouse is free to use the income from both Trusts. Once both partners are deceased, the beneficiaries of their respective Trusts will inherit the funds, hopefully with no federal or state Estate Tax due. If the couple does not set up a Trust and continues to hold all of their property jointly, the last to die will own the two million dollars with only one Estate Tax Exclusion available.

☆☆ AVOID APPOINTMENT OF A GUARDIAN

Once you have a Trust, you do not need to worry about who will take care of your property should you become disabled or too aged to handle your finances. The person you appoint as Successor Trustee will take over the care of the Trust property if you are unable to do so. If you do not make provision for the care of your property in the event of your incapacity, it may be necessary for a Court to appoint a Guardian of your property. Guardianship is a good thing to avoid, not only because of the cost of the procedure, but also to avoid the embarrassment of a Court coming to the conclusion that you are unable to manage your own finances.

Before appointing a Guardian, the Court will have you examined and will conduct a hearing to determine whether you are a **disabled person** as defined by Illinois statute (755 ILCS 5/11a-2) (i.e., that you are not fully able to manage your person or property). If he finds that you cannot manage your finances, he will appoint a Guardian of your property. To protect your assets, the judge will require that the Guardian obtain a bond.

Once appointed, the Guardian will take possession of your property and file an inventory with the Court. The Guardian will manage your property and regularly account to the Court for monies spent. (755 ILCS 5/11a-3, 5/11a-18, 5/14-1, 5/24-11). He may need to employ an accountant to assist with these reports. The Guardian needs to employ an attorney to establish the Guardianship and see to it that it is properly administered. The Guardian, and his attorney, are entitled to be paid for their efforts on your behalf (755 ILCS 5/27-1, 5/27-2).

Court filing fees, the cost of a bond, accounting fees, Guardian's fees, attorney's fees for you and the Guardian, are all paid from your Estate (that's your money!). And this expense goes on year after year until you are restored to capacity or die (755 ILCS 5/24-19).

Putting your assets in a Living Trust can avoid all this.

☆ CARE FOR FAMILY MEMBER

You can make provision in your Trust to care for a minor child or family member after you die. If your beneficiary is a minor, you can direct your Successor Trustee to distribute the child's inheritance at different times. For example, you can direct your Successor Trustee to give the beneficiary a certain amount of money when he is 18, then 21, then 25, then 30, and so on.

If your intended beneficiary has a creditor problem, you can set up a **Spendthrift Trust** to protect the Trust funds from the claims of creditors (735 ILCS 5/2-1403, 760 ILCS 5/15.1). You can direct your Successor Trustee to spend Trust funds for your beneficiary's health care, education, and living expenses, and nothing more. With a properly drafted Spendthrift provision the Trust funds will be protected from the creditors of the beneficiary — with an important exception: the monies can be used for child support.

Under Illinois law, if a Grantor sets up a Trust for the benefit of someone, regardless of whether it is a Spendthrift Trust, or not, the income to which the beneficiary is entitled is available to pay for monies he owes for child support. If beneficiary is the sole beneficiary of the Trust, the Court can require that Trust property (i.e., the *principal* of the Trust) be used to pay for back child support payments (735 ILCS 5/2-1403).

NO CREDITOR PROTECTION FOR SETTLOR

You can set up a Spendthrift Trust for a beneficiary, but not for yourself. Because property held in your Revocable Living Trust is freely accessible to you, it is likewise accessible to your creditors both before and after your death. If you die owing money, your creditors can have a Personal Representative appointed to locate funds to pay those debts. The Personal Representative can require that your Trust property be used to pay for those debts (755 ILCS 5/16-1, 16-2). If your creditor knows of the Trust, he can sue to have your debt paid from the Trust funds without the need to have a Personal Representative appointed (760 ILCS 15/6(a), 15/6(f)).

☆ PRIVACY

Your Living Trust is a private document. No one but your Successor Trustee and your beneficiaries need ever read it. If you leave property in a Will and there is a Probate procedure, the Will must be filed with the court, where it becomes a public document. Anyone can go to the courthouse, read your Will and see who you did (or did not) provide for in your Will. Records in the Probate Court (inventories, creditor's claims, etc.) are open to public scrutiny. In some states, Court records are now available on the Internet!

LEASE SAFE DEPOSIT BOX AS TRUSTEE

One of the benefits of having a Living Trust is that you can lease the safe deposit box in your name as Trustee. When you lease the safe deposit box you can have an agreement with the bank that they are to allow your Successor Trustee free access to the safe deposit box in the event of your incapacity or death.

This protects your privacy. As explained in Chapter 3, if you hold the safe deposit box in your name only, the bank will restrict access to the box as soon as they learn of your death. They will not allow anyone to take possession of the contents of your box without a Court order, however, as explained on page 85, any interested party, can ask the bank to be allowed to examine the contents of the box to see if your Will is there (755 ILCS 15/1).

By leasing a safe deposit box as Trustee, only you and your Successor Trustee need ever know of the contents of the box.

THE PROBLEMS

With all these perks, you may be ready to call your attorney to make an appointment to set up a Trust, but before doing so there are a few things you need to consider:

☒ COMPLEXITY

A Trust is a fairly complex document, often 20 pages long. It needs to be that long because you are establishing a vehicle to take care of your property during your lifetime, as well as after your death. The Trust usually is written in "legalese," so it may take you considerable time and effort to understand it. It is important to have your Trust document prepared by an attorney who has the patience to work with you until you fully understand each paragraph of the document and are satisfied that what it says is what you really want.

☒ COST

Because of the thoroughness of the document and the fact that it is custom designed for you, a Trust will cost much more to draft than a simple Will. In addition to the initial cost of the Trust, it can be expensive to maintain the Trust should you become disabled or die. Your Successor Trustee has the right to charge a reasonable compensation for his duties as Trustee, as well as to charge for any specialized services he performs. A financial institution can charge to serve as Successor Trustee, and also charge to manage the Trust portfolio (760 ILCS 5/7). If you decide to have a financial institution serve as Trustee, then it is important that you compare the fee schedules of different institutions.

You can choose an attorney, or an accountant, or a financial planner, to serve as Trustee, but this may create a conflict of interest because the professional can use his position as Trustee to generate fees. If you decide to appoint a professional as Trustee you should have a fee agreement stating what will be charged for his duties as Trustee and what will be charged for professional work done on behalf of the Trust. The fee agreement should be included in the Trust document with a provision that whoever accepts the job of Successor Trustee, agrees to accept the fee as provided in the Trust document.

You may decide to appoint your spouse or a family member as Successor Trustee, who may want little, or no, compensation. Regardless of who you choose to be Successor Trustee, you need to come to a fee agreement. The agreement can be for a set amount or a percentage of the value of the Trust, or other method to be used to determine his compensation.

☒ YOU MAY NEED YOUR SPOUSE'S PERMISSION TO TRANSFER PROPERTY INTO YOUR TRUST

Most married couples prepare a Trust as part of their overall Estate Plan. Sometimes a married person has a Trust that was prepared prior to the marriage, or he may decide to create a Trust to care for children from a previous marriage. In such case, it may be prudent to have the spouse agree, in writing, to transfers into the Trust.

Permission is recommended because of the right of a surviving spouse to inherit property under Illinois law. Regardless of whether a married person dies with or without a Will, the surviving spouse is entitled to be supported in his/her accustomed manner from the decedent's Estate for up to 9 months from the date of death. In addition to this spousal support, the surviving spouse is entitle to at least one-third of the Estate of the deceased spouse. If the decedent dies without a Will, the surviving spouse is entitled to at least half his Probate Estate. If the decedent's Will provides for less than this **Statutory Share**, the surviving spouse can renounce the Will and demand the amount provided by Illinois law (755 ILCS 5/2-1, 5/2-8, 5/15-1).

The astute reader might question what happens if there is no Probate. Suppose all of the decedent's property is held in his Trust. If the decedent made no provision for his spouse in his Trust, doesn't that deprive the spouse of the right to a Statutory Share? Illinois Courts have ruled that if a person's Estate is held in non-Probate assets (such as Trust property) so that it deprives the surviving spouse of his/her rights under Illinois law, the Courts can, after examining all of the circumstances, require those assets be used to provide those statutory rights (*Montgomery v. Michaels*, 54 Ill.2d. 532 (1973), 301 N.E.2d 465, and *In Re Estate of Caffrey*, 120 Ill. App.3 917 (1983), 458 N.E.ed 1147).

☒ PROBATE MIGHT STILL BE NECESSARY

The Trust only works for those items that you place in the Trust. If you own property in your name only, then upon your death, a Probate procedure might be necessary in order to transfer the property to your beneficiary. For example, if you purchase a security in your name only, without a "Transfer On Death" designation to a named beneficiary or to your Trust, then a Probate procedure may be necessary to determine who should inherit the security.

The attorney who prepares the Trust usually creates a safety net for such situations. He prepares a Will for you to sign at the same time you sign the Trust. The Will makes your Trust the beneficiary of your Probate Estate. If you own anything in your name only and a Probate procedure is necessary, the Will directs your Personal Representative to make that asset part of your Trust by transferring the asset to your Successor Trustee. Your Successor Trustee will add that asset to your Trust (755 ILCS 5/4-4).

The Will prepared by the attorney is called a **Pour Over Will** because it is designed to "pour" any asset titled in your name only, into the Trust. Having the Will ensures that all of your property will go to the beneficiaries named in your Trust. But the downside of holding property in your name only is that a full Probate procedure may be necessary just to get that asset into your Trust. If avoiding Probate is your goal, holding property in your name only, defeats that goal.

You can ensure that a Probate procedure will not be necessary by transferring your assets into your Trust during your lifetime, but if you neglect to put something into your Trust, the Pour Over Will stands by to transfer that asset into your Trust.

☒ TAXES MAY STILL BE A PROBLEM

While you are operating the Trust as Trustee, all of the property held in your Revocable Living Trust is taxed as if you were holding that property in your own name. If the value of your Trust property exceeds the Estate Tax Exclusion value, taxes will be due and owing once you die. If all you own is held in your Trust, your Successor Trustee will need to pay those taxes from the Trust property.

Those who have Estates large enough to incur Estate Taxes also need to think about how taxes will be paid on other taxable transfers. For example, suppose you and your brother bought a home as Joint Tenants With Right of Survivorship. If you each contributed equally to the purchase, and the property is now worth one million dollars, your brother will inherit your half million dollar share. If you also own two million dollars in other property all of which is in your Trust, your Taxable Estate is $2,500,000.

Unless your Trust directs otherwise, each beneficiary of your Estate is responsible to pay a proportionate share of the Estate Taxes. If federal Estate Taxes are reinstated so that anything over one million dollars is taxable at a rate of 40%, your Estate Tax will be $600,000. Your brother will need to contribute his prorated share of the Estate Taxes:
$500,000/$2,500,000 = .2
20% of $600,000 = $120,000.

But suppose your brother doesn't have that kind of cash? Should he be forced to sell his home in order to pay the taxes? Should your Successor Trustee use your Trust property to pay your brother's taxes with a promise that he will reimburse the beneficiaries of your Trust at a later date? An experienced Estate Planning attorney can suggest any number of ways to head off such problems.

⊠ ☆ THE TRUST IS LEGALLY ENFORCEABLE

Your Successor Trustee will take over the administration of your Trust upon your incapacity or death. Should there be a dispute regarding the administration of the Trust, your beneficiary (or your Successor Trustee) can petition the Court to settle the matter. For example, your Successor Trustee is entitled to reasonable compensation. If you did not set the amount he is to be paid in the Trust Agreement and the beneficiaries object to the amount he is charging, they can ask the Court to determine his compensation (760 ILCS 5/7).

We gave this section a cross and a star because the right to have a Trust enforced or administered by the Court is a double edged sword. It is great to have the Court protect the rights of your beneficiaries, but the cost of a court battle could be greater than if your Estate was Probated and the money simply distributed to your beneficiaries.

The beneficiaries of your Trust are at a financial disadvantage in a dispute with your Successor Trustee. The Court can require your Trustee to be personally liable for his legal costs, but that only happens if the Trustee acted illegally or unreasonably. In most cases, the Trustee will be able to charge the expense of defending his actions to your Trust and your beneficiaries will pay for their legal expenses out of their own pockets.

Win or lose, there will be just that much less for your beneficiaries to inherit.

MAYBE PROBATE ISN'T ALL THAT BAD

Although all of the methods discussed in this Chapter can be used to transfer property without the need for Probate, each method may have a downside that is objectionable to you. Maybe you don't have enough money to warrant the cost of setting up the Trust at this time. Holding property jointly with another may raise issues of security and independence. Holding property so that it goes directly to a few beneficiaries in a Pay On Death account may not be as flexible as you wish.

This is especially the case if you wish to give gifts to several charities or to minor children instead of just one or two beneficiaries. For example, if you hold all your property so that it goes to your son without the need for Probate, and you ask him to use some of the money for your grandchild's education, it may be that your grandchild gets none of the money because your son is sued or falls upon hard times. If you keep your property in your name only and leave a Will giving a certain amount of money for your grandchild, the child will know exactly how much money you left and the purpose of that gift.

After taking into account all the pros and cons of avoiding Probate, you may well opt for a Will and a Probate procedure. If you make such a decision, it is important to keep in mind that Estate Planning is not an "all or nothing" choice. You can arrange your Estate so that certain items pass automatically to your intended beneficiary, and other items can be left in your name only, to be distributed as part of a Probate procedure. By arranging your finances in this manner, you can reduce the value of your Probate Estate, and that in turn should reduce the cost of Probate.

Your Illinois Will   8

Many people decide that the Will is the best route to go but do not act upon it, thinking it unnecessary to prepare a Will until they are very old and about to die. But according to reports published by the National Center for Health Statistics (a division of the U.S. Department of Health and Human Services) 2 of every 10 people who die in any given year are under the age of 60.

Twenty percent may seem like a small number until it hits close to home as it did with a young couple. They were having difficulty conceiving a child. They went from doctor to doctor until they met someone just beginning his practice. With his knowledge of the latest advances in medicine, he was able to help them.

The birth of their child was a moment of joy and gratitude. They asked a nurse to take a picture of them all together — the proud parents, the newborn child and the doctor who made it all possible. Happiness radiated from the picture, but within 6 months, one of them would be dead.

You might think it was the child. An infant's life is so fragile. SIDS and all manner of childhood diseases can threaten a little one. No, he grew up a healthy young man.

If you looked at the picture, you might guess the husband. Overweight and stressed out, his ruddy complexion suggested high blood pressure. He looked like a typical heart-attack-prone Type A personality.

No, he was fine and went on to enjoy raising his son.

Probably it was the wife. She had such a difficult time with the pregnancy and the delivery was especially hard. Maybe it was all too much for her.

No, she recovered and later had two more children.

It was the doctor who was killed in a collision with a truck.

WHY A WILL IS NECESSARY

Though we all agree that one never knows, still people put off making a Will figuring that if they die before getting around to it, Illinois law will take over and their property will be distributed in the manner that they would have wanted anyway. The problem with that logic is the complexity of the Illinois Laws of Descent and Distribution. If you are survived by a spouse, child, parent or sibling, it isn't too difficult to figure out who will inherit your property. But if none of these survive you, the ultimate beneficiary of your property may not be the person you would have chosen, had you taken the time to do so.

Others think that it is not necessary to have a Will because they arranged their finances so that all of their property will be inherited without the need for Probate. But money could come into your Estate after your death. This could happen in any number of ways. You might die in a house fire, or a flood. Your insurance company may need to pay for damages done to your home. You might be killed in a car accident caused by the wrongful act of someone. In such case, a Personal Representative may need to be appointed to sue on behalf of your Estate.

As explained in Chapter 6, without a Will, the Court will use an order of priority as set by Illinois law to appoint a Personal Representative. The person chosen by the Court may not be the person you would have chosen to settle your Estate. And as we will see in this Chapter, there are other important reasons to make a Will.

📄 SET THE PERSONAL REPRESENTATIVE'S FEE

An important reason to make a Will is so that you can choose your Personal Representative and come to an understanding about how much compensation he/she is to receive. You can state that value in your Will.

CAUTION THE PERSONAL REPRESENTATIVE CAN SEEK MORE MONEY

You can put the amount of agreed compensation in your Will; however your Personal Representative can reject that amount as not being reasonable compensation and ask the Court to set a greater amount. To avoid the problem, you can have your attorney draft an Agreement that you and your Personal Representative sign and attach it to your Will.

Having a separate fee Agreement will not stop your Personal Representative from asking for more money, but with such an Agreement, generally, the Court will not agree to the increase unless something unusual occurs (such as a law suit) causing much more work than the ordinary Probate procedure.

You also need to keep in mind that the Personal Representative's fee is just to administer the Estate. It does not include payment for professional work he may do while settling the Estate. For example, if you appoint your attorney as Personal Representative, he can agree to the amount stated in the Will for his role as Personal Representative, and then ask the Court to award him attorney's fees as well (755 ILCS 5/27-1, 5/27-2). The same goes for any other professional. If you appoint your accountant as your Personal Representative, he is entitled to receive compensation for his work as Representative and also for any accounting work he does such as preparing tax returns and settlement statements for the beneficiaries.

A financial planner who serves as Personal Representative may be compensated for his management of the Estate property (buying and selling securities, taking care of rental property, etc.) in addition to his fee to administer the Estate.

But the main problem with appointing a professional as your Personal Representative is the same as appointing a professional to serve as the Successor Trustee of your Trust; namely, that it creates a potential conflict of interest. The professional can use his position as Personal Representative to generate fees that may not have been necessary had someone else settled the Estate.

When choosing a Personal Representative, consider the relationship of the Personal Representative to the beneficiaries and determine whether it would be better to appoint a non-professional for the job

CHOOSE A GUARDIAN FOR YOUR MINOR CHILD

If one parent dies, then it is the right, and duty, of the surviving parent to care for the child. But it could happen that both parents become incapacitated or die before the child is grown. If you have a minor child, you have the right to name someone to serve as the Guardian of your child in the event that both you and the other parent are deceased. You can do so by means of a separate writing, or you can include an appointment of Guardian in your Will (755 ILCS 5/11-5, 5/11-5.3).

You can even include a Trust provision in your Will, naming someone to serve as Trustee to care for property that you leave to your minor child. See Chapter 7 for more information about how to provide for the care of your minor child in the event of your incapacity or death.

MAKE GIFTS OF YOUR PERSONAL PROPERTY

Another benefit to making a Will is that you can make gifts of your personal property, including your car. If you make a gift of your car in your Will, it will be relatively simple for your car to be transferred to the beneficiary. If you do not make a *specific gift* of your car, it becomes part of your Probate Estate. Your Personal Representative will decide what to do with the car. He can sell it and include the proceeds of the sale in the Estate funds to be distributed to your residuary beneficiaries; or he can give the car to one beneficiary of your Estate as part of that beneficiary's share of the Estate.

SMALL GIFTS MATTER

Many who have lost someone close to them report that the distribution of small personal items caused the greatest conflict. If you arrange your finances so that no Probate procedure is necessary, your next of kin will need to decide how to distribute your personal effects. Without guidance from you and no Personal Representative with authority to make decisions, there could be disagreement and hard feelings, over items of little monetary value. If you make a Will, you can include a list of gifts of personal effects in your Will and your Personal Representative will distribute the gifts according to your directions.

Of course, you cannot list each and every item you own, but you can instruct your Personal Representative to allow certain family members to take their choice of items not mentioned in your Will. If two or more family members want the same item, have your Personal Representative use an appropriate lottery system (coin toss, high card in a cut of a deck of cards, etc.) to decide who "wins."

📄 MAKE ADJUSTMENT FOR PRIOR GIFTS

You can use your Will to make adjustments for gifts or loans given during your lifetime. For example, if you have loaned money to a family member and do not expect to be repaid, you can deduct the loan from that person's inheritance. There is no need to make the adjustment if the borrower gives you a promissory note because should you die, the monies will be owed to your Estate and the Personal Representative can deduct the monies owed from the borrower's inheritance. But if there is no evidence of the debt and you neglect to make a Will, the borrower will receive whatever is allowed under the Laws of Descent.

That was the case with Sally and Tom and their four children. They were firm believers in treating each of their children equally. "Share and share alike" was their favorite saying. Once Tom died, Sally continued with the tradition.

Sally did not think of the loan she gave to her son as a gift. After all, he promised to pay it back, with interest! She did not ask her son to sign a promissory note. He was family. If you can't trust your son, who can you trust?

The son was prompt with his monthly payments. But only two payments had been made before his mother died suddenly, from a heart attack. Sally never mentioned the loan to any of her other children. Neither did her son.

Each child received one quarter of their mother's Estate; and no one the wiser. Except whenever Sally's son dreams of his mother, she is not smiling.

📄 MAKE PROVISION FOR PAYMENT OF DEBTS AND TAXES

If you owe money on your home, car, or other property, unless you make some other provisions in your Will, the beneficiaries of that item, will inherit the loan along with the gift. This s so regardless of whether the inheritance was through a Probate or non-Probate transfer. For example, if you own property jointly, the surviving joint owner will be responsible to pay the debt (755 ILCS 5/20-19).

Taxes are another concern for those Estates large enough to be subject to Estate taxes. Federal law require that Estate Taxes be paid by the beneficiaries of the Estate in proportion to the value received, unless the decedent made some other arrangements to pay for the taxes. If you make no provision for the payment of taxes, whoever inherits your property will pay a percentage of the taxes based on the amount they receive (26 U.S.C. 6324 (a)(2)).

If this is not as you wish you can direct your Personal Representative to pay all of your debts and taxes from your Probate Estate. If you do so, those who inherit property from a non-Probate transfer will not contribute to the payment of your debts and taxes. All of the money you owe will be paid from your Probate Estate. This means that the amount your residuary beneficiaries receive will be reduced by the amount of paid for debts and taxes.

CHOOSE THE TYPE OF ADMINISTRATION

It is fairly common practice in Illinois for a Will maker to include directions in his Will allowing his Personal Representative to conduct an Independent Administration, i.e., without Court supervision. An Independent Administration generally reduces the cost of the administration because the Personal Representative can settle the Estate without having an attorney file a petition seeking Court approval for his actions.

The beneficiaries are free to challenge any of his actions in Court, or even to ask the Court to supervise the administration. However, if you direct an Independent Administration, the Court will not grant a request for a Supervised Administration, unless there is some good reason to do so (755 ILCS 5/28-4).

It is also common practice for a Will maker to waive bond so that his beneficiaries will not need to pay for the cost of the Personal Representative's bond. If you waive bond, your beneficiaries have the right to ask the Court to order the Personal Representative be bonded. The judge will grant the request, or order bond on his own, should he determine that there is a need to protect Estate property (755 ILCS 5/12-4).

PREPARING AND STORING THE WILL

A Will may look like a simple document, but it takes a certain amount of legal expertise to write it in a manner that will give effect to your wishes. Your Will needs to be clearly worded so there is no doubt about what you intended. A sentence that can be read in two different ways can lead to a dispute over what you intended; and that could result in a long and expensive Court battle.

You need to make provision for alternate beneficiaries, in the event a beneficiary dies before you. If the alternate beneficiary is a minor, you need to give directions about how to keep the gift safe until the child is grown. An attorney can suggest different ways to protect the gift.

As explained in Chapter 5, there are any number of ways to challenge the Will, if it is not properly signed and witnessed. If the challenge is successful, the Court may refuse to admit the Will to Probate, and your property will be distributed as if there were no Will at all (755 ILCS 5/4-3). If you want to be assured that your Will is honored, it is best to have an Estate Planning attorney prepare and then supervise the signing of your Will.

STORING THE WILL

Once you sign your Will, you may wonder where to store it. Your attorney may suggest that he place it in his vault for safekeeping. By doing so, he ensures that your heirs will need to contact him as soon as you die. This does not mean that they are required to employ him should a Probate proceeding be necessary. It only means that he will have an opportunity for future employment.

But there are problems with such an arrangement. The Will could be lost or mistaken for another Will. That happened in at least one case. The attorney prepared Wills for two people with the same name and similar family circumstances. When one person died the attorney submitted the wrong Will to Probate. Luckily the error was quickly discovered. The decedent had a distinctive signature. The family challenged the validity of the Will based on the unfamiliar signature and the way the property was to be distributed. They knew the decedent would not have distributed his property in the manner stated in the Will.

If you decided to allow your attorney to store your original Will, you need assurances that the attorney will be responsible for the document. You should get a receipt and something in writing that says:

➪ The attorney accepts full responsibility for the storage of the Will. Should it be lost or damaged, he will redraft the document for you to sign, and at no cost to you. If you are deceased, he will, at no cost to your heirs, present sufficient evidence to the Court to accept a valid copy of the Will into Probate.

➪ There will be no charge to you, or your heirs, for the storage and retrieval of the document.

➪ Should he sell his practice, retire, or die, he or the successor to his practice, will return the original document to you.

THE SAFE DEPOSIT BOX — SAFE BUT . . .

You might consider placing your Will in a safe deposit box that you lease at a bank. The only problem with the bank safe deposit box is convenient access. If you hold a safe deposit box in your name only, should you die, the bank will restrict access to the safe deposit box as soon as they are notified of your death.

As explained on page 85, the bank may allow an "interested party" to inspect the contents of your safe box provided they do so under the supervision of an officer or employee of the company (755 ILCS 15/1). If your Will is there, they will forward it to the Probate Court, but they will not allow anything else to be removed without Court permission. Once a Personal Representative is appointed by the Court, he will have such authority and be able to remove the contents of the safe deposit box. But if you arranged your finances to avoid Probate, it is self defeating to have entry to a safe deposit box trigger a Probate procedure.

For those who are happily married, the solution to the problem of accessing the safe deposit box after death, may be to lease the box jointly with your spouse such that each of you has free access to the box. However, this may not be the best solution if you think your spouse will be unhappy with certain provisions made in your Will. Some Wills never see the light of day for that reason.

As explained in Chapter 7, those who have a Trust can solve the problem by giving their Successor Trustee joint access to the safe deposit box. If you do not have a Trust, you can lease the box jointly with a trusted family member. But if privacy and security are important to you, this might offset any concern for the convenience of your beneficiaries. In such case, consider keeping the document in a fireproof safe deposit box within your home. You can give a duplicate key to the person you chose to be your Personal Representative.

Regardless of where you choose to store your Will, let your Personal Representative know that you have a Will and how to retrieve it in the event of your death.

CHOOSING THE RIGHT ESTATE PLAN

Joint Ownership?
A Pay On Death bank account?
A Transfer On Death Security?
A Will?
A Trust?
A Life Insurance Policy???

Chapters 7 and 8 offer so many options that the reader may be more confused than when he was blissfully unenlightened.

As with most things in life, you may find there are no ultimate solutions, just alternatives. The right choice for you is the one that best accomplishes your goal. This being the case, you first need to determine what you want to accomplish with the money you leave. Think about what will happen to your property if you were to die suddenly, without making any plan different from the one you now have.

> Who will be responsible to pay your bills?
> Who will inherit your property?
> Will Probate be necessary?

If the answers to these questions are not as you wish, you need to work to arrange your property to accomplish your goals.

For those with significant assets — especially those with Estates large enough to pay Estate taxes — a trip to an experienced Estate Planning attorney may be well worth the consultation fee.

Your Estate Plan Record   9

Once you are satisfied with your Estate Plan, then the final thing to consider is whether your heirs will be able to locate your assets once you are gone.

Most people have their business records in one place, their Will in another place, car titles and deeds in still another place. When someone dies, their beneficiaries may feel as if they are playing a game of "hide and seek" with the decedent. The game might be fun were it not for the fact that an unlocated item may be forever lost. For example, suppose you die in an accident and no one knows you are insured by your credit card company for accidental death in the amount of $25,000. The only one to profit is the insurance company, which is just that much richer because no one told them that you died as a result of an accident.

And how about a key to a safe deposit box located in another state? Will anyone find it? Even if they find the key, how will they find the box?

It is not difficult to arrange things so that your affairs are always in order. It amounts to being aware of what you own (and owe) and keeping a record of your possessions. A side benefit is that by doing so, you will always know where all your business records are. If you ever spent time trying to collect information to file your taxes or trying to find a lost stock or bond certificate, you will appreciate the value of organizing your records.

ORGANIZING YOUR RECORDS

Heirs need all the help they can get. It is difficult enough dealing with the loss, without the frustration of trying to locate important documents. Your heirs will have no problem locating your assets if you keep all of your records in a single place. It can be a desk drawer or a file cabinet or even a shoe box. It is helpful if you keep a separate file or folder for each type of investment. You might consider setting up the following folders:

📁 THE BANK & SECURITIES FOLDER

Store your original certificates for stocks, bonds, mutual funds, certificates of deposit, in a folder labeled **BANK & SECURITIES**. In addition to the original certificate include a copy of the contract you signed with each financial institution. The contract will show where you have funds and who you named as beneficiary or joint owner of the account. If someone owes you money and signed a promissory note or mortgage identifying you as the lender, store these documents in this folder as well.

If you have a safe deposit box, keep a record of its location and the number of the box. Keep a copy of all of the items stored in the box in this folder. If you have an extra key to the box, put it here.

E-bank Accounts If you are doing your banking on-line, it is important to keep a record of your passwords so that your family can access the account in the event of your incapacity or death. The same applies if you have on-line brokerage or installment loan accounts. Keep a paper record of these accounts in this folder.

📁 THE INSURANCE FOLDER

The **INSURANCE FOLDER** is for each insurance policy that you own, be it life insurance, car insurance, homeowner's insurance or a health care insurance policy. If you purchased real property, you probably received a title commitment at closing and the title insurance policy some weeks later when you received your original deed from recording. If you cannot locate the title insurance policy, then contact the closing agent and have him send you a copy of your title policy.

📁 THE PENSION AND ANNUITY FOLDER

If you have a pension or annuity, then put all of the documents relating to the pension in this folder. Include the telephone number and/or address of the person to contact in the event of your death.

FOR FEDERAL RETIREES If you are a federal retiree, you should have received your **PERSONAL IDENTIFICATION NUMBER** (**PIN**) and the person who will inherit your pension (your *survivor annuitant*) should have his/her own PIN as well. It is relatively simple to obtain this during your lifetime, but it may be difficult and/or stressful for your survivor annuitant to work through the system once you are gone.

Survivor annuitant benefits are not automatic. Your survivor annuitant must apply for them by submitting a death claim to the Office of Personnel Management. Your survivor needs to know that it is necessary to apply and also how to apply. You can get printed information about how to apply for benefits from the Office Of Personnel Management (see Page 34). Keep the printed information in this file.

📁 THE DEED FOLDER

Many people save every scrap of paper associated with the closing of real property. If you closed recently on real estate and there was a mortgage involved in the purchase, you probably walked away from closing with enough paper to wallpaper your kitchen. If you wish, you can keep all of those papers in a separate file that identifies the property, for example:

CLOSING PAPERS FOR THE PEORIA PROPERTY

Place the original deed (or a copy if the original is in a safe deposit box) in a separate **DEED FOLDER**. Include cemetery deeds, condominium deeds, cooperative shares to real property, timesharing certificates, deed to out of state property, etc. Also include a copy of related documents such as an Abstract of Title, or a recorded Condominium Approval. If you have a title insurance policy, put the original in the insurance folder, and a copy in this folder. If you have a mortgage on your property, put a copy of the recorded mortgage and promissory note in a separate **LIABILITY FOLDER**.

LOCATING REAL PROPERTY

If you own a vacant lot, your beneficiaries will find the deed (or a copy) in this folder but that deed will not contain the address of that property because it doesn't have one. The post office does not assign a street address until there is a building on the site. Your beneficiaries can get the location of the property from city or county records. But why make things hard for them? Include a handwritten note in this folder that tells them exactly how to locate the property.

📁 THE LIABILITY FOLDER

The LIABILITY FOLDER should contain all loan documents of debts that you owe. For example, if you purchased real property and have a mortgage on that property, put a copy of the mortgage and promissory note in this folder. If you owe money on a car, put the loan documents in this folder. If you have a credit card, put a copy of the contract you signed with the credit card company in this folder. A lease is a liability, because you contracted to pay a certain amount for the period of the lease, so include a copy of any lease agreement in this folder.

If you have a mortgage on your property, put a copy of the recorded mortgage and promissory note in a this folder. Once the mortgage is paid off, the lender should give you a *Mortgage Certificate of Release* (765 ILCS 905/2). In some states is it referred to as a *Satisfaction of Mortgage*. The Release needs to be recorded in the county where the property is located. Keep the recorded Release together with the deed to the property. Remember to remove the paid mortgage from your Liability Folder.

Many people never take the time to calculate their net worth (what a person owns less what that person owes). By having a record of your assets and outstanding debts, you can calculate your net worth whenever you wish.

📁 THE PERSONAL PROPERTY FOLDER

MOTOR VEHICLES

Put all motor vehicle titles in a Personal Property folder. This includes cars, mobile homes, boats, planes, etc. If you owe money on the vehicle, the lender may have possession of the title certificate. If such is the case, put a copy of the title certificate and registration in this folder and a copy of the loan documents in a separate liability folder.

If you own a boat or plane, identify the location of the motor vehicle. For example, if you are leasing space in a marina, or in an airplane hangar, keep a copy of the leasing agreement in this file.

JEWELRY

If you own expensive jewelry, keep a picture of the item together with the sales receipt or written appraisal in this folder.

COLLECTOR'S ITEMS

If you own a valuable art or coin collection, or any other item of significant value, include a picture of the item in this file. Also include evidence of ownership of the item, such as a sales receipt or a certificate of authenticity, or a written appraisal of the property.

📂 THE PERSONAL RECORDS FOLDER

The **PERSONAL RECORDS FOLDER** should include documents that relate to you personally, such as a birth certificate, naturalization papers, marriage certificate, divorce papers, military records, Social Security card, etc. If you have a Power of Attorney For Health Care, or a Living Will, or a Power of Attorney for Finances, you can place the document in this folder, or in your Estate Planning folder. If you placed the original document in a safe deposit box, keep a copy in this folder together with the location of the original.

📂 THE ESTATE PLANNING DOCUMENT FOLDER

Place your Estate Planning documents (Will, Trust, Premarital Agreement, burial, funeral arrangements, etc.) in a separate folder. If your attorney has your original documents, or you placed the original in a safe deposit box, place a copy of the document in this folder together with instructions about how to find the original.

It is important to keep a copy of your Will or Trust because over the years you may forget what provision you made. Keeping a copy in your home may save you a trip to the safe deposit box to determine whether you need to update the document.

📁 THE TAX RECORD FOLDER

Your Personal Representative (or next of kin) will need to file your final income tax returns. Keep a copy of your tax returns (both federal and state) for the past three years in your **TAX RECORD FOLDER**.

As explained in Chapter 2, beginning in 2010, there will be a cap on the step-up basis to 4.3 million dollars for property inherited by the spouse and 1.3 million dollars for property inherited by anyone else. It is important to keep a record of the basis of your property, not only for your heirs, but for yourself should you decide to sell the property during your lifetime. If you purchase real property, you need to keep a record of the purchase price as well as monies you paid to improve the property. For condominium units, that will include special assessments for improvements to the property.

You will need these records to determine whether there will be a Capital Gains Tax on the transfer. Your accountant can help you set up a bookkeeping system to keep a running record of your basis in everything you own of value.

THE *If I Die* FILE

Many do not have the time, nor inclination, to "play" with all these folders. They do not anticipate an immediate demise. Getting hit by a truck, or dying in a fiery plane crash is not something to think about, much less prepare for. But consider that death is not the only problem. You could take suddenly ill (say with a stroke) and become incapacitated. Even the most time-starved optimist should have a murmur of concern that his loved ones will be left with a mess should something unforeseen happen.

If you do not feel like doing a complete job of organizing your records at this time, consider an abridged version. You can set up a single file with a list of all you own and the location of each item. You need to make that file easily accessible to whomever you wish to manage your affairs in the event of your incapacity or death. You can do this by letting that person know of the existence of the file and how to get it in an emergency; or keep the file in an easily accessible place in your home with the succinct but attention-grabbing title of *"If I Die."*

We have included a form on the next page that you can use as a basis for information to be included in the file.

If I Die

the following information will help settle my Estate:

INFORMATION FOR DEATH CERTIFICATE

MY FULL LEGAL NAME _____
MY SOCIAL SECURITY NO. _____
MY USUAL OCCUPATION _____
BIRTH DATE AND BIRTH PLACE _____
If naturalized, date & place _____
MY FATHER'S NAME _____
MY MOTHER'S MAIDEN NAME _____

PEOPLE TO BE NOTIFIED

_____
_____
_____

FUNERAL AND BURIAL ARRANGEMENTS

LOCATION OF BURIAL SITE

_____

LOCATION OF PRE-NEED FUNERAL CONTRACT

_____

FOR VETERAN or SPOUSE BURIAL IN A NATIONAL CEMETERY

BRANCH_____SERIAL NO._____
VETERAN'S RANK _____
VETERAN'S VA CLAIM NUMBER _____
DATE AND PLACE OF ENTRY INTO SERVICE:
_____
DATE AND PLACE OF SEPARATION FROM SERVICE:
_____
LOCATION OF OFFICIAL MILITARY DISCHARGE
OR DD 214 FORM_____

LOCATION OF LEGAL DOCUMENTS

BIRTH CERTIFICATE _____
MARRIAGE CERTIFICATE_____
PREMARITAL AGREEMENT _____
DIVORCE DECREE _____
PASSPORT _____
WILL OR TRUST _____
DEEDS _____
MORTGAGES _____
TITLE TO MOTOR VEHICLES _____
POWER OF ATTORNEY _____
Attorney name & telephone _____

LOCATION OF FINANCIAL RECORDS

INSURANCE POLICIES:
Name of Company, Location of Policy, Insurance Agent
_____
_____

PENSIONS/ANNUITIES:
IF FEDERAL RETIREE: PIN NUMBER: _____
NAME OF SURVIVOR _____
SURVIVOR PIN NUMBER _____

BANK
Name and address of Bank, Account Number,
Location of Safe Deposit Box and Key
_____
_____

SECURITIES
Name and telephone number of broker
_____

TAX RECORDS FOR PAST THREE YEARS
LOCATION _____
Accountant name and telephone number
_____

KEEPING UP TO DATE

We discussed people's natural disinclination to make an Estate Plan until they are faced with their own mortality. Many believe that they will make just one Will and then die (maybe that's why they put off making a Will). The reality is, most people who make a Will change it at least once before they die. If you have an Estate Plan, it is important to update it when any of the following events take place:

✍ CHANGE IN MARITAL STATUS
GETTING MARRIED

In the early 20th century, marriage was a simple thing. Two young people fell in love, and married. There was no need for a *Premarital Agreement* because they came to the marriage with little property and an intent to stay together "till death do us part." Today, many postpone marriage until they have established careers, so they come into the marriage with property that they worked hard to acquire. The intent to remain married remains, but young people are realistic. They know the statistics. Half of the marriages don't work out. But, ever optimistic, the majority of those who divorce will re-marry at least once and in many cases, with children from a prior union.

It is a foolhardy couple who enter a marriage in today's society without a Premarital Agreement that spells out the rights and responsibilities of the couple in the event that one of them dies, or they divorce. Courts in Illinois will enforce the agreement, provided the document was prepared according to Illinois law, i.e., the document was signed voluntarily after full disclosure of the finances of each party (750 ILCS 10/7). A document that is too one-sided can be challenged in Court, so it is important that both parties be represented by their own attorney.

Once the honeymoon is over, it is important to examine your pre-marriage Estate Plan. As explained in Chapter 5, if you do not change the Will you signed before you married, your spouse may be able to challenge that Will, unless your Premarital Agreement gives up statutory rights as they apply to married people.

You should review your Premarital Agreement on a regular basis as your finances change or as you have children. With the consent of your spouse, you can amend your Agreement. If it needs a complete revision, you can revoke the Agreement, and replace it with a Post-marital Agreement (750 ILCS 10/6).

Changes to the original agreement need to be prepared and signed in the same manner as your original agreement. There must be full disclosure by both parties as to the extent of their wealth. Each should be represented by his own attorney.

GETTING DIVORCED

If your marriage is annulled or you are divorced, certain changes take place by law. For example, If you have a Will or Trust and neglect to change the document after the divorce, should you die, any provision relating to your spouse will be read as if the spouse died on the day you were divorced (755 ILCS 5/4-7, 760 ILCS 35/1(a)).

Title to your home is also affected by divorce. Unless the final judgment of dissolution says differently, there no longer is any Right of Survivorship in homestead property owned by you and your spouse. The property becomes a Tenancy-In-Common by operation of law.

But it is important to not just rely on the law because the law may change, or there may be exceptions in the law that are unknown to you. For example, current law provides that if you divorce and afterward decide to live together in some other property as your homestead, then each spouse has rights of survivorship in that property (765 ILCS 1005/1c). Best to change all documents after the divorce. That includes deeds, Wills, Powers of Attorney, beneficiaries of insurance policies, pension plans, etc.

✍ A CHANGE IN RELATIONSHIP

If you marry, separate, divorce, have a child, or if a beneficiary of your Estate dies, you need to examine your Will to determine whether it needs to be revised. It is important to have changes made by a properly drafted and signed document. If you make changes by crossing things out or writing over your Will, the validity of the document can be challenged once you die.

If you decide that your Will needs a complete revision, it is important to have a new Will prepared. Simply ripping up the old Will effectively revokes the Will (755 ILCS 5/4-7(a)). But it could happen that someone (perhaps your attorney) has a copy of the Will. If no one knows that you revoked the Will, they may think the Will is lost and then offer the copy of the Will for Probate (see page 84). If you draft a new Will, the first paragraph should say, "I revoke all prior Wills ..."

NOTIFY EMPLOYER OF CHANGE

If you change your marital status (either marry or divorce), you need to tell your employer of the change so that the employer can change your status for purposes of paycheck tax deductions. If you have a health insurance plan or a pension plan that provides benefits to your spouse, these need to be changed as well.

BENEFICIARY MOVES OR DIES

Most people remember to name an alternate beneficiary should one of their beneficiaries die. But how many of us remember to notify the pension plan or insurance company when a beneficiary moves? Many life insurance proceeds are never paid because the company cannot locate the beneficiary. The Actuarial Office of the Federal Employees' Group Life Insurance Program reported that as of September, 2003, they had over 55.8 million dollars in unpaid benefits, mostly because they could not locate the beneficiary at the last given address.

✍ RELOCATION TO A NEW STATE OR COUNTRY

There is no need to change your Estate Plan for a move within the state of Illinois. There is much to check out if you are moving to another state. If your attorney has your original Will (or any other original document), then unless you plan to continue with him as your attorney, you need to retrieve those originals and take them with you to the new state.

You need to determine whether your Will conforms to the laws of the state of your new residence. Most states will honor a Will drafted according to Illinois law, however, the rights of a spouse vary considerably state to state. If you are married and have not provided the minimum amount as required by the laws of the new state, should you die before your spouse, your Will may be challenged on that basis. The same applies to a Trust. Many states require funds from a Revocable Living Trust be used to pay the minimum amount allowed by law to the surviving spouse.

If you do not have a Will, it is important to check out the Laws of Descent and Distribution for that state. In some states they are called the Laws of Intestate Succession Each state has its own laws of inheritance of property and those laws are different state to state. Who has the right to inherit your property in the state of Illinois may differ from who can inherit your property in another state. If you do not have a Will, this is the time to think about who will inherit your property should you die in the state of your new residence.

This is especially important for those who are married. The right of a spouse to inherit property varies significantly from state to state. There is a world of difference in the rights of a spouse in a Community Property state (Arizona, California, Idaho, Louisiana, Nevada, New Mexico, Texas, Washington and Wisconsin) and other states. There is even variation in the rights of a spouse from one Community Property state to another!

OTHER ESTATE PLANNING DOCUMENTS
A Medical or **Health Care Directive** is a document that gives instructions about the health care the person signing the document (the *Principal*) wants to receive in the event that he is too ill to make his own medical decisions. In Illinois, that document is called a **Power of Attorney For Health Care** and the person appointed to carry out your health care instructions, your **Health Care Agent.** If you have a Power of Attorney For Health Care, you need to determine whether it will be effective in the state of your new residence. Under Illinois law, a Power of Attorney for Health Care that is executed according to the laws of another state, is valid here in Illinois (755 ILCS 45/2-4(b)). But not all states have laws requiring doctors in that state to rely on a document drafted in another state. But even if the laws of the state honor your Illinois Power of Attorney for Health Care, consider drafting another in the new state.

Health Care Directives vary significantly state to state. Other states may have laws that enable you to appoint someone with powers similar to a Health Care Agent, but the laws of the state may refer to such person as a *Patient Advocate* or a *Health Care Surrogate* or a *Health Care Representative.* It is best to sign a new Health Care Power of Attorney using the form and terminology recognized in the new state, rather than chance any confusion should you become ill and find yourself in an emergency situation.

Similarly, if you have appointed someone to handle your finances under a Power of Attorney, you may want to have another prepared in conformity with the laws of the new state, so there will be no question of the right of your Agent to conduct business on your behalf.

CREDITOR PROTECTION

Creditor protection is another item that is significantly different state to state. If you have much debt, then determine what items can be inherited by your family free of your debts.

TAX CONCERNS

You also need to check out the taxes of the new state. Each state has its own tax structure. Some states have an inheritance tax, or a transfer tax on all inherited property. If state taxes are high, you may need an Estate Plan that will minimize the impact of those taxes.

When moving to another state you need to either educate yourself about the laws of the state, or consult with an attorney who can assist you in reviewing your Estate Plan to see if that plan will accomplish your goals in that state.

✎ A SIGNIFICANT CHANGE IN THE LAW

A major problem associated with the legal system in the United States is its volatility. Changes might be easy to keep up with if we had only one set of laws. But we are ruled by federal statutes and regulations and state statutes and regulations. We pay state and federal legislators to make laws and change existing statutes and regulations. We pay judges to tell us the meaning of the law, but their interpretation of the law may change the way the law operates. The legislature and the judiciary do their job and so laws and regulations change frequently and often without prior notice.

We, the public, are charged with the duty of understanding the law. Many a citizen has been chided with "Ignorance of the law is no excuse." Most of us have a general concept of what is and what is not allowed in our society, however, when presented with a particular problem, we may need to turn to a professional (lawyer, accountant, journalist, city official, etc.) to get an explanation of the law.

Areas of the law that affect you and your family, personally, are discussed in this book, namely Probate Law, Tax Law, and Estate Planning (Wills and Trusts). It is important to keep up with news in these areas to learn about changes in the law that may affect your Estate Plan. It is a good idea to check with your attorney on a regular basis to determine whether you need to change your Will or Trust because of a change in state or federal law.

Also check out the Eagle Publishing Company Web site for changes we will post to keep this book fresh.
http://www.eaglepublishing.com

GAMES DECEDENTS PLAY

We discussed the game of "hide and seek" some decedents play with their heirs. A variation of that game is the "wild goose chase." The person who plays this game is one who never updates his files. His records are filled with all sorts of lapsed insurance policies, promissory notes of debts long since paid; brokerage statements of securities that have been sold, and so on.

When he is gone, his family will become frustrated as they try to hunt down the "missing" asset. If you wish to play this game, then the best joke is to keep the key to a safe deposit box that you are no longer leasing. That will keep folks hunting for a long time!

If you do not have a wicked sense of humor, then do your family a favor and update your records on a regular basis.

Glossary

ABSTRACT OF TITLE An *Abstract of Title* is a condensed history of the title to the land. It consists of a summary of all the documents.

ADMINISTRATION The *Administration* of a Probate Estate is the management and settlement of the decedent's affairs. There are different types of administration. See *Ancillary Administration* and *Summary administration.*

ADMINISTRATIVE LAW JUDGE An *Administrative Law Judge* is someone who is appointed to conduct an administrative hearing. He has the power to administer oaths, take testimony, and then decide the facts of the case. Although he can decide the facts of the case, the final outcome of the hearing is decided by the government agency that appointed the Administrative Law Judge.

AFFIANT An *Affiant* is someone who signs an affidavit and swears or acknowledges that it is true in the presence of a notary public or other person with authority to administer an oath or take acknowledgments.

AFFIDAVIT An *Affidavit* is a written statement of fact made by someone voluntarily, under oath, or acknowledged as being true, in the presence of a notary public or someone else who has authority to administer an oath or take acknowledgments.

AGENT An *Agent* is someone who is authorized by another (the *principal*) to act for or in place of the principal.

ANATOMICAL GIFT An *Anatomical Gift* is the donation of all or part of the body of the decedent for the purpose of transplantation or research.

ANCILLARY ADMINISTRATION An *Ancillary Administration* is a Probate proceeding that aids or assists the original (primary) Probate proceeding. Ancillary administration is conducted in another state to determine the beneficiary of the decedent's property located within that state, and to determine whether the property is taxable in that state.

ANNUAL GIFT TAX EXCLUSION The *Annual Gift Tax Exclusion* is the amount a person can gift to another each year without being required to file a federal Gift Tax Return. The Annual Gift Tax Exclusion is currently $11,000, but is expected to increase to $12,000 in the year 2006.

ANNUITANT An *annuitant* is someone who is entitled to receive payments under an annuity contract.

ANNUITY An *annuity* is a contract that gives someone (the annuitant) the right to receive periodic payments (monthly, quarterly) for the life of the annuitant or for a given number of years.

ASSET An *asset* is anything owned by someone that has a value, including personal property (jewelry, paintings, securities, cash, motor vehicles, etc.) and real property (condominiums, vacant lots, acreage, residences, etc.).

ASSIGN To *assign* is to transfer one's rights in or to something to another. For example, a contract may allow a party to assign his rights in the contract to another person.

ATTORNEY or ATTORNEY AT LAW An *attorney*, also known as an *Attorney at law*, or a *lawyer*, is someone who is licensed by the state to practice law in that state.

ATTORNEY-IN-FACT An *Attorney-In-Fact* is someone appointed to act as an Agent for another (the Principal) under a Power of Attorney.

BASIS The *basis* is a value that is assigned to an asset for the purpose of determining the gain (or loss) on the sale of the item or in determining the value of the item in the hands of someone who has received it as a gift.

BENEFICIARY A *beneficiary* is one who benefits from the act of another or from the transfer of property. In this book we refer to a beneficiary as someone named in a Will, Trust, or deed to receive property, or someone who inherits property under the Laws of Intestate Succession.

BOND A *bond* required by the Probate Court is a written document that guarantees the Personal Representative will perform his duties as required by law. The person or company that insures the performance of the Personal Representative is called a *surety.* The value of the bond is set by the Court. The cost of purchasing the bond is charged to the decedent's Estate.

CAPITAL GAINS TAX A *Capital Gains Tax* is a tax on the amount the net sales proceeds exceeds the basis of a capital asset sold by a taxpayer.

CAVEAT *Caveat* is Latin for "Let him beware." It is a warning for the reader to be careful.

CFR *CFR* is the abbreviation for the *Code of Federal Regulations.*

CLAIM A *claim* against the decedent's estate is a demand for payment of a debt of the decedent. To be effective, the claim must be filed with the Probate Court within the time limits set by law.

CODE A *Code* is a body of laws arranged systematically for easy reference, e.g. the Internal Revenue Code.

GLOSSARY *253*

COLUMBARIUM A *Columbarium* is a separate room or building with niches (spaces) designed to store urns containing the ashes of cremated bodies.

COMMISSIONER A *Commissioner* is someone appointed by the Court or by the government to do a job.

COMMON LAW MARRIAGE A *Common Law marriage* is one that is entered into without a state marriage license or any kind of official marriage ceremony. A Common Law marriage is created by an agreement to marry, followed by the two living together, and telling everyone they know that they are husband and wife. Illinois does not recognize a Common Law marriage unless it was entered into in another state that considers the union to be a valid marriage.

COMMUNITY PROPERTY   Certain states (Arizona, California, Idaho, Louisiana, Nevada, New Mexico, Texas, Washington, and Wisconsin) have laws stating that property acquired by husband or wife, or both, during their marriage is *Community Property* and is owned equally by both of them.

CONTINGENT BENEFICIARY A *Contingent Beneficiary* is an alternate beneficiary; i.e. someone who inherits if the primary beneficiary dies or loses the right to inherit.

CONFLICT OF INTEREST A *conflict of interest* is a conflict between the official duties of a fiduciary (Guardian, Trustee, attorney, etc.) and his own private interest. For example, it is a conflict of interest for a Successor Trustee to use Trust property for his own personal profit.

DEED OF TRUST A *Deed of Trust* is a deed that places title to real property in Trust to secure payment of monies owed on the property. It serves the same function as a mortgage.

COURT The *Court* as used in this book is the Probate Court. When referring to an order made by the court, the term is synonymous with "judge," i.e., an "order of the court" is an order made by the judge of the court.

CREDITOR A *creditor* is someone to whom a debt is owed by another person, the *debtor*.

CREMAINS *Cremains* is shorthand for *cremated remains*. It refers to the ashes of a person who was cremated.

CURTESY *Curtesy* is the right of a husband, upon the death of his wife, to a life estate in real property she owned during their marriage, provided they had a surviving child who could inherit the property. This English Common Law has been abolished in most states, including Illinois.

CUSTODIAN A *Custodian* under the *Illinois Uniform Transfers to Minors Act* is a person or a financial institution that accepts responsibility for the care and management of property given to a minor child.

DAMAGES *Damages* is money that is awarded by a Court as compensation to someone who has been injured by the action of another.

DEBTOR A *debtor* is someone who owes payment of money or services to another person (the *creditor*).

DECEDENT The *Decedent* is the person who died.

DESCENDANT A *descendant* is someone who descends from a common ancestor. There are two kinds of descendants: a *lineal descendant* and a *collateral descendant*. The lineal descendant is one who descends in a straight line such as father to son to grandson. The collateral descendant is one who descends in a parallel line, such as a cousin. In this book, unless otherwise stated, the term *descendant* refers to a *lineal descendant*.

DISABLED The term *disabled* is used in two ways. A person is *physically disabled* or *incapacitated* if he lacks the ability to perform certain tasks. A person is *legally disabled* if a Court rules that he is unable to care for his person or property.

DISTRIBUTION The *distribution* of a Trust or Probate Estate is the giving to the beneficiary that part of the Estate to which the beneficiary is entitled.

DURABLE POWER OF ATTORNEY A ***Durable Power of Attorney*** is a document in which the person who signs the document (the *Principal*) gives another person (his *Attorney in Fact*) authority to do certain things on behalf of the Principal. The Attorney in Fact is also referred to as the Principal's *Agent*. The word *"durable"* means that the authority of the Agent continues even if the Principal is incapacitated at the time that the Agent is acting on behalf of the Principal.

EQUITABLE *Equitable* is whatever is right or just. If property is distributed to two or more people equitably, then the division is not necessarily equal, but according to the principles of justice or fairness.

EQUITY The *equity* in a home is the market value of the home less monies owed on the property (mortgages, tax liens, etc.).

ERISA *ERISA* is the abbreviation for the Employee Retirement Income Security Act. This federal law governs the funding, investment, administration and termination of private pension plans.

ESTATE A person's *Estate* is all of the property (both real and personal property) owned by that person. The decedent's Estate may also be referred to as his *Taxable Estate* because all of the decedent's assets must be included when determining whether Estate Taxes are due. Compare to PROBATE ESTATE.

EXECUTOR An *Executor* (feminine *Executrix*) is a legal term found in many Wills. The terms refer to the person appointed by the Will maker to carry out directions given in the Will. In modern Wills, this term has been replaced by *Personal Representative.*

FIDUCIARY A *Fiduciary* is one who takes on the duty of holding property in Trust for another or acting for the benefit of another, such as a Personal Representative, Trustee, Guardian etc.. A fiduciary relationship is also one that is developed out of trust and confidence. For example, an attorney has a fiduciary relationship with his client.

GRANTEE   The *Grantee* of a deed is the person who receives title to real property from the *Grantor*.

GRANTOR The *Grantor* is someone who transfers property. The Grantor of a deed is the person who transfers real property to a new owner (the Grantee). The Grantor of a Trust is someone who creates the Trust and then transfers property into the Trust. Also see SETTLOR.

GUARANTOR A *Guarantor* is someone who promises to pay a debt or perform a contract for another person in the event that person does not fulfill his obligation.

GUARDIAN A *Guardian* is someone who has legal authority to care for the person and/or property of a minor or someone who has been found by the Court to be disabled.

HEALTH CARE AGENT A *Health Care Agent* is someone who is appointed by another (the *Principal)* to make medical decisions on behalf of the Principal, in the event that the Principal is to too ill to speak for himself.

HEALTH CARE DIRECTIVE A *Health Care Directive* is a statement made by someone (the *Principal)* in the presence of witnesses or a written, notarized statement in which the principal gives directions about the care he/she wishes to receive. See **Living Will** and **Power of Attorney for Health Care**.

HEIR An *heir* is anyone entitled to inherit the decedent's property under the Laws of Descent and Distribution in the event that the decedent dies without a Will.

HOLOGRAPHIC WILL A *Holographic Will* is a Will written, dated and signed by the hand of the Will maker himself. Many states, including Illinois, refuse to admit a Holographic Will into Probate unless it is witnessed according to the laws of the state.

HOMESTEAD The *homestead* is the dwelling and land owned and occupied as the owner's principal residence.

ILCS *ILCS* is the abbreviation for the *Illinois Compiled Statutes*.

INDEPENDENT ADMINISTRATION An *Independent Administration* is a probate procedure that is conducted with minimal court supervision.

INDIGENT   A person who is *indigent* is one who is poor and without funds.

IRA ACCOUNT An *Individual Retirement Account ("IRA")* is a retirement savings account in which income taxes on certain deposits and interest to the account are deferred until the monies are withdrawn.

IRREVOCABLE TRUST An *Irrevocable Trust* is a Trust that cannot be changed, cancelled or terminated until its purpose is accomplished.

INSOLVENT A person or business is *insolvent* if more money is owed than owned, or if the person or business is unable to pay debts as they come due.

INTER VIVOS TRUST   An *Inter Vivos Trust* (also known as a *Living Trust*) is a Trust that is created and becomes effective during the lifetime of the Grantor (or Settlor) as opposed to a Trust that he includes as part of his Will to take effect upon his death.

INTESTATE *Intestate* means not having a Will or dying without a Will. *Testate* is to have a Will or dying with a Will.

JOINT AND SEVERAL LIABILITY   If two or more people agree to be *jointly and severally liable* to pay a debt, then each individually agrees to be responsible to pay the debt, and together they all agree to pay for the debt.

JOINT TENANCY In Illinois, a *Joint Tenancy* means that each tenant owns an equal share of the property. There is no right of survivorship in real property unless the deed specifically says that the Joint Tenants do not own the property as Tenants In Common. This differs from a bank account or a car owned jointly in Illinois. Unless title to the car or the bank account states different, each joint owner has a right of survivorship.

KEY MAN INSURANCE *Key man insurance* is an insurance policy designed to protect a company from economic loss in the event that an important employee of the company becomes disabled or dies.

LAWS OF DESCENT AND DISTRIBUTION The *Laws of Descent and Distribution* (also known as the *Laws of Intestate Succession*) are the laws of the state that determine who is to inherit the decedent's Probate Estate if the decedent died without a valid Will.

LEGALESE *Legalese* refers to the use of legal terms and confusing text that is used by some attorneys to draft legal documents.

LEGATEE A *Legatee* is a person to whom a legacy (gift) is given in a Will, as compared to an *Heir* who receives an inheritance under the Laws of Intestate Succession. For simplicity we have used the term *Beneficiary* for both Legatees and Heirs.

LESSOR A *Lessor* is a person or company who leases property to another (the *Lessee*). In the case of real property, the Lessor is known as the Landlord and the Lessee as the Tenant.

LETTERS *Letters* is a document, issued by the Probate court, giving the Personal Representative authority to take possession of and to administer the Estate of the decedent.

LIEN A *lien* is a charge against a person's property as security for a debt. The lien is evidence of the creditor's right to take the property as full or partial payment, in the event that the debtor defaults in paying the monies owed.

LIFE ESTATE A *Life Estate* interest in real property is the right to possess and occupy the property for so long as the owner of the Life Estate lives. When the owner of the Life Estate dies, the property will belong to the owner of the ***Remainder Interest***.

LITIGATION *Litigation* is the process of carrying on a lawsuit, i.e., to sue for some right or remedy in a court of law. A Litigation Attorney is one who is experienced in conducting the lawsuit and in particular, going to trial.

LIVING WILL A *Living Will* is a Health Care Directive that gives instructions about whether life support systems should be withheld or withdrawn in the event that the person who signs the Living Will is terminally ill or in a persistent vegetative state and unable to speak for himself.

MEDICAID *Medicaid* is a public assistance program sponsored jointly by the federal and state government to provide Medical Assistance for people with low income and limited assets.

NET PROBATE ESTATE The *net Probate Estate* is the value of the decedent's Probate Estate, less all the monies paid to settle the Estate, i.e. what is left once all taxes, valid claims and the costs and expenses of administration are paid.

NET PROCEEDS The *net proceeds* of a sale is the sale price less costs and expenses paid to make the sale.

NET WORTH A person's *net worth* is the value of all of the property that he owns less the monies he owes.

NEXT OF KIN *Next of kin* has two meanings in law: *next of kin* refers to a person's nearest blood relation or it can refer to those people (not necessarily blood relations) who are entitled to inherit the property of a person who dies without a valid Will.

NON-PROBATE TRANSFER A *non-Probate Transfer* is the transfer of property to the decedent's beneficiary without the need for Probate. This includes property that is transferred to a surviving joint owner, or property transferred to the beneficiary of a Pay On Death account.

PERJURY *Perjury* is lying under oath. The false statement can be made as a witness in Court or by signing an Affidavit. Perjury is a criminal offense.

PERSONAL EFFECTS *Personal effects* is personal property that is kept for one's personal use such as clothing, jewelry, books, and other items generally found in the home.

PERSONAL PROPERTY *Personal property* is all property owned by a person that is not real property (real estate). It includes personal effects, cars, securities, bank accounts, insurance policies, etc.

PERSONAL REPRESENTATIVE A *Personal Representative* is someone appointed by the Probate Court to settle the decedent's Estate and to distribute whatever is left to the proper beneficiary.

PER STIRPES *Per Stirpes* is a method of distributing property to a group of beneficiaries. In the event a beneficiary dies before the gift is distributed, the deceased person's share goes to his descendants. If he has no descendants, the surviving beneficiaries share equally in the gift.

PETITION A *Petition* is a formal, written request to a Court asking the Court to take action or issue an order on a given matter; e.g. a request to appoint a Guardian.

POSTNUPTIAL AGREEMENT A *Postnuptial Agreement* is an agreement made by a couple after marriage to decide their respective rights in case of a dissolution or the death of a spouse.

POWER OF ATTORNEY A *Power of Attorney* is a document in which someone (the *Principal*) gives another person (his *Agent* or *Attorney-In-Fact*) authority to do certain things on behalf of the Principal. A **Power of Attorney For Health Care** is a document giving the Agent authority to make health care decisions for the Principal in the event the Principal is too ill to do so himself.

PREMARITAL AGREEMENT A *Premarital Agreement* is an agreement made prior to marriage whereby a couple determines how their property is to be managed during their marriage and how their property is to be divided should one die, or they later divorce.

PRINCIPAL The *Principal* of a Power of Attorney is the person who permits or directs another (his **Attorney-In-Fact** or *Agent*) to act for him.

PROBATE *Probate* is a Court procedure in which a Court determines the existence of a valid Will. The Decedent's Estate is then settled by the Personal Representative who pays all valid claims and then distributes whatever remains to the proper beneficiary.

PROBATE ESTATE The *Probate Estate* is that part of the decedent's Estate that is subject to Probate. It includes property that the decedent owned in his name only or as a Tenant-In-Common. It does not include property that was jointly with right of survivorship. It does not include property held "in trust for" or "for the benefit of" someone.

PRO BONO The term *Pro Bono* means "for the public good." When an attorney works Pro Bono, he does so voluntarily and without pay.

PUNITIVE DAMAGES *Punitive damages* are awarded by a Court to punish someone who deliberately disregarded the rights or safety of another. It is money awarded in addition to *compensatory damages* which are monies awarded to reimburse the wronged person for actual losses.

QRP *QRP* is the abbreviation for a *Qualified Retirement Plan*. This is a plan authorized under federal law, in which income taxes on certain deposits and interest to the account are deferred until the monies are withdrawn.

REAL PROPERTY *Real property*, also known as *real estate*, is land and anything permanently attached to the land such as buildings and fences.

REGISTERED AGENT   A *Registered Agent* of a corporation is someone who is authorized to act on behalf of the company and accept service of process in the event the company is sued.

REMAINDER INTEREST The *Remainder Interest* in real property is the property that passes to the owner of that Interest, once the owner of the Life Estate dies. See LIFE ESTATE.

REPARATION   *Reparation* is money paid to make up for an injury or wrongdoing

RESIDUARY BENEFICIARY A *Residuary Beneficiary* of a Will is a beneficiary who is entitled to whatever is left of the Probate Estate once specific gifts have been distributed and the decedent's bills, taxes and costs of Probate have been paid. Unless the Will makes some other provision, Residuary Beneficiaries share equally in the Residuary Estate.

RESIDUARY ESTATE The *Residuary Estate* is whatever is left of the Probate Estate once specific gifts made in the Will have been distributed and once the decedent's bills, taxes and costs of Probate have been paid.

REVOCABLE TRUST   A *Revocable Trust* is a Trust which can be amended or revoked by the Settlor during his lifetime.

REVOCABLE LIVING TRUST A *Revocable Living Trust* (also known as an *Inter Vivos Trust*) is a Revocable Trust that is created and becomes effective during the lifetime of the Settlor.

RIGHT OF SURVIVORSHIP A *Right of Survivorship* is the right of the survivor of a deceased person to the property of the decedent.

SECURED LOAN A *Secured loan* is a loan backed by property. If the borrower does not pay the debt, the lender can take the property. Car loans and mortgages are secured loans.

SETTLOR   A *Settlor* (also known as a *Grantor*) is someone who creates and then funds a Trust.

SIBLING A *sibling* is one of two or more people born of the same parents; i.e., a brother or a sister. Unless, otherwise noted, we used the term to include those who have only one parent in common; i.e. a half brother or a half sister.

SOLEMNIZE   To *solemnize* a marriage is to enter a marriage publicly, before witnesses, rather than privately as in a Common Law marriage.

SPECIFIC GIFT A *Specific Gift* is a gift of a specific item, or part of the Will maker's Estate, that is made to a named beneficiary of the Will.

SPENDTHRIFT   A *spendthrift* is someone who spends money carelessly or wastefully or extravagantly.

SPENDTHRIFT TRUST   A *Spendthrift Trust* is a Trust created to provide monies to a beneficiary, and at the same time protect the Trust property from being taken by the creditors of the beneficiary.

STATUTE OF LIMITATION A *Statute of Limitation* is a federal or state law that sets maximum time periods for taking legal action. Once the time set out in the statute passes, no legal action can be taken.

STEPPED-UP BASIS A *stepped-up basis* is the value placed on property that is acquired in a taxable transaction such as inheriting property or purchasing property (Internal Revenue Code 1014). The "step-up" refers to the increase in value from the basis of the former owner (usually what he paid for it), to the basis of the new owner (usually the market value when the transfer is made).

SUCCESSOR TRUSTEE A *Successor Trustee* is someone who takes the place of the Trustee.

SUMMARY ADMINISTRATION A *Summary Administration* is a simplified and/or shortened Probate procedure.

SUPERVISED ADMINISTRATION *A Supervised Administration* is a Probate procedure that requires the Personal Representative to seek Court approval before taking certain actions.

SURETY BOND A *Surety Bond* is a bond in which a company (the *Surety*) agrees to pay if the *Principal* defaults on his obligation. For example, if the Court orders the Personal Representative to be bonded and he does not perform his duties causing the Estate to lose money, the Court can require the Surety to pay for lost funds.

SURROGATE A *Surrogate* is a substitute; someone who acts in place of another.

TENANCY BY THE ENTIRETY   A *Tenancy by the Entirety* is the name of a form of ownership of real property held by a husband and wife. It is a joint tenancy with right of survivorship, modified by the common law concept that the husband and wife are one. With a joint tenancy with right of survivor, each joint tenant owns their own share of the property until death, when the surviving owner owns it 100%. With a Tenancy by the Entirety, each owns 100% of the property both before and after death.

TENANCY IN COMMON   *Tenancy In Common* is a form of ownership such that each Tenant owns his share without any claim to that share by the other Tenants. There is no right of survivorship. Should a Tenant In Common die, his share belongs to the Tenant's Estate and not to the surviving owners of the property.

TESTATE *Testate* means having made a Will or dying with a Will.

TESTATOR   The *Testator* is someone who makes and signs a Will; or someone who dies leaving a Will.

TITLE INSURANCE   *Title Insurance* is a policy issued by a title insurance company after searching title to the property. The insurance covers losses that result from a defect of title, such as unpaid taxes, or a claim of ownership of the property.

TOTTEN TRUST ACCOUNT   A *Totten Trust Account* is a bank account that is held in trust for a beneficiary. The terms of the Trust are established through agreement with the bank, and not through a separate Trust Agreement.

TRUST AGREEMENT A *Trust Agreement* is a document in which someone (the *Settlor* or *Grantor*) creates a Trust and appoints a *Trustee* to manage property placed into the Trust. The usual purpose of the Trust is to benefit persons or charities named by the Grantor as beneficiaries of the Trust.

TRUSTEE   A *Trustee* is a person, or institution, who accepts the duty of caring for property for the benefit of another.

UNDUE INFLUENCE   *Undue influence* is pressure, influence or persuasion that overpowers a person's free will or judgment, so that a person acts according to the will or purpose of the dominating party.

WAIVER   A *waiver* is the intentional and voluntary giving up of a known right.

WARRANTY DEED A *Warranty Deed* is a deed in which the Grantor warrants (promises) that the property he is transferring has good and clear title; i.e., that no one else has rights in the property. This is different than a *Quit-claim Deed* where the Grantor says, in effect, "I am releasing any interest I have in this property to you, but I make no guarantees about anyone else's right to this property."

WRONGFUL DEATH   A *wrongful death* is a death that was caused by the willful or negligent act of a person or company.

INDEX

A

AARP 83

ABANDONED PROPERTY 75, 76

ABSTRACT OF TITLE 71, 234

ACCIDENT INSURANCE 47, 54

ACCOUNTING
180, 195, 206, 207

ADOPTED CHILD 135

ADMINISTRATION
Ancillary 81, 202
Full 172
Independent 173
Small Estate 164-167
Summary Administration
170, 171, 188
Supervised 173
To Collect 26

ADMINISTRATIVE LAW JUDGE
102

ADVANCE BENEFICIARY NOTICE
100

ADVERTISER 55

AFFIDAVIT 86, 87, 164-168

AFTERBORN CHILD 136

AIRCRAFT 70, 161

ALL-TERRAIN VEHICLE 68, 156

AMBIGUOUS DEED 122

AMERICAN COUNCIL
OF LIFE INSURERS 48

ANATOMICAL GIFT 5-8, 21

ANCESTORS 130

ANCILLARY ADMIN. 81, 202

ANNUAL GIFT TAX EXCLUSION
38, 199

ANNUITIES 34, 35, 104, 139, 233

APPRAISAL 179, 236

ATTORNEY FEE 83, 178

AUTHORIZING AGENT 14

AUTOMOBILE
(see Motor Vehicle)

AUTOPSY 2-4

271

B

BANK ACCOUNT
- Beneficiary — 57, 190, 193
- E-Bank — 66, 232
- Insurance — 47
- In Trust For — 127, 190, 192
- Joint — 93, 189, 191
- Multiple Party — 189
- Out of State — 74
- Ownership — 189
- POD — 190, 215, 229
- Transfer — 152
- Unclaimed — 75

BASIS, step up — 41, 199, 238

BENEFICIARY
- Alternate — 56, 138, 139, 226
- Change of — 56, 57, 244
- Contingent — 56
- Of Bank Account — 57, 190, 193
- Of Homestead — 43
- Of Motor Vehicle — 154
- Of Pension Plan — 57
- Of Trust — 44, 117, 204
- Of Will — 56
- Residuary — 154, 222
- Rights — 174-182

BILLS (see Debts)

BOND — 171, 176, 177, 206, 207, 225

BROKERAGE ACCOUNTS (See SECURITIES)

BURIAL
- Out of State — 18
- Problem — 25
- Military — 19-21
- Transit Permit — 11, 17, 18

BUSINESS
- Ownership — 49, 69
- Records — 62, 69

C

CAPITAL GAINS TAX — 41, 42, 186, 197, 238

CAR (see MOTOR VEHICLE)

CASKETS — 12-14, 17

CEMETERY, Military — 19

CENTERS FOR MEDICARE AND MEDICAID — 52

CERTIFICATE
- Of Release — 235
- Of Title — 159

CHECK LIST — 183-185

CHECKS — 64

CHILD
- Adopted — 135
- Afterborn — 136
- Award — 109
- Dependent — 107, 108, 137
- Disabled — 33, 103
- Minor — 21, 24, 33, 107-109, 137, 165, 193-195, 221
- Non-marital — 137
- Rights of — 135-137

272   Guiding Those Left Behind In Illinois

CLAIMS (See CREDITOR)		CREMAINS	8, 18
COBRA	53, 54	CRIME VICTIM	23
COLUMBARIUM	17	CUSTODIAN	194, 195

D

DEATH
  Accidental   47
  Certificate   11, 18, 27, 28, 86
                                    149, 153, 159, 164
  Simultaneous   138
  Wrongful   22, 105

COMMON LAW MARRIAGE	130		
COMMUNITY PROPERTY			
	125, 202, 246		
COMPUTER	66		
CONDO APPROVAL	234		
CONTRACT	79		

DEBTS
  Credit Card   27, 45
  Joint   92, 93
  Owed to decedent   115
  Spouse   89-92

CONTINGENT BENEFICIARY	56	DEED	71, 121-126
			128, 168, 196, 234
CORONER	3, 4	DEPEND.& INDEM. COMP.	21
CORPORATION	50		
COST OF ADMINISTRATION	110	DESCENDANTS	130
COUNTY		DISABLED PERSON	206
Assessor	43, 157		
Recorder	169	DIVORCE	20, 123, 144
			189, 197, 242-244
COURT DOCUMENTS	186	DIRECT MKETING ASSOC.	55
CREDIT CARD DEBT	27, 45	DOCTRINE OF NECESS.	89-91

CREDITOR
  Claim   58, 89, 103, 150
  Notice To   58, 97, 171, 166
  Protection   104-109, 208, 247

		DONOR CARDS	5, 8
CREMATION	14-18	DOWER RIGHTS	125

INDEX   ***273***

DRIVER SERVICE DEPT   150

E

ELDER LAW ATTY   96, 200, 201

EMBALMING   11, 12

ERISA   104

ESTATE
  Administration   30
  Plan   187
  Tax   38-41, 81, 121, 181
    199, 202, 205, 224, 229

EXECUTOR   6, 26, 80, 114

EXEMPT PROPERTY   107, 150

F

FEDERAL
  Aviation Admin.   70
  Estate Tax   38-41, 81, 121
    181, 199, 202, 205, 224, 229
  Retiree   34, 233
  Statutes   (see STATUTES)
  Trade Commission Rules
    (see STATUTES)

FEES
  Attorney   83, 207, 210
  Custodian   195
  Guardian   207
  Personal Representative
    177, 220
  Trustee   210

FIDUCIARY   73

FINANCIAL RECORDS   66

FUNERAL
  Arrangements   10, 11, 237
  Directors   3, 11, 12, 18
  Expense   110, 146, 164
  On-line   13
  Problem   25

G

GIFT
  Of Personal Prop.   222
  Of Real Property   196-201
  Prior   222
  Specific   135, 222, 224
  Tax   38, 40, 138
  To Minor   193-195

GOV'T PENSIONS   34, 233

GRANTEE OF DEED   121, 196

GRANTOR
  Of Deed   121
  Of Trust   44, 56, 203

GUARANTOR   92, 96

GUARDIAN   6, 24, 193, 201
    206, 193, 221

H

HALF BLOOD   130, 133

HEALTH CARE
  Agent   246
  Directive   246, 247

HEALTH INSURANCE   52-54

HOLOCAUST   76

HOLOGRAPHIC WILL	141

HOMEOWNER'S INSURANCE 51

HOMESTEAD
  Capital Gains Exclusion   42
  Creditor Protection   109, 198
  Gift Of   197-201
  Tax Credit   198
  Tax Exemption   43

I
IF I DIE FILE   239-241

ILLINOIS
  Agency (see STATE AGENCY)
  Statutes (see STATUTES)
  Web Sites (see WEB SITES)

INCOME TAX
  Return   37, 43, 73, 198
  Refund   77, 162, 163

INDEPENDENT ADMINISTRATION
    173, 175, 180, 225

INHERITANCE TAX   202, 247

INSURANCE
  Accident   47
  Beneficiary of   56, 138
  Health   52-54
  Key man   49
  Life 4, 47, 56, 105, 138, 139, 245
  Lost Policy   48
  Motor Vehicle   46
  Mortgage   51
  Title   71, 233, 234
  Work Related   49

INTESTATE SUCCESSION
    132, 246

INTER VIVOS TRUST   203

IN TRUST FOR ACCOUNT
    127, 190, 192

INVENTORY   179, 206

IRA ACCOUNT   36, 57, 104

IRREVOCABLE
  Gift   194
  Trust   204

IRS FORMS
  Form 56   73
  Form 1040   37, 162
  Form 1099   74
  Form 1310   162
  Form 4506   73

J
JOINT
  Account   93, 189, 191
  Debts   92, 93
  Property 93, 117-122, 125, 138
    159, 188, 189, 196
  Tenants 122, 123, 188, 192, 196

K
KEYS   62, 63, 231, 249

KEY MAN INSURANCE   49

KILLER   139

L

LAWYER, how to find   xiii-xv

LAWS OF DESCENT
See RULES OF DESCENT

LAWS OF INTESTATE SUCCESSION
    132, 246

LEASED
  Car   67, 158
  Mobile home lot   68, 157
  Residence   69

LEGAL AID   xiv

LETTERS   29

LIFE
  Estate   124, 168, 169, 201, 202
  Insurance   4, 47, 56, 105
    138, 139, 245

LIMITING CHARGE   99

LIVING TRUST   203

M

MAIL   62, 63

MANUFACTURED HOME
    68, 157

MARRIAGE   129-131, 242, 244

MARRIED WOMAN'S
  RIGHTS   90

MEDICAID   103, 200

MEDICAL EXAMINER   3, 4

MEDICARE
  Advance Bene. Notice   100
  Appeal   102
  Assignment   99
  Billing   98-101
  Coverage   52
  Fraud   98
  Limiting Charge   99
  Medigap   101
  Spouse's Coverage   53
  Summary Notice   98

MILITARY BURIAL   19-21

MINOR CHILD   21, 24, 33
    107-109, 137
    165, 193-195, 221

MISSING BODY   26

MOBILE HOME   68, 157

MORTGAGE
  Insurance   51
  Satisfaction of   235

MOTORBOATS   76, 159

MOTOR VEHICLE
  Gift   222
  Held In Trust   127
  Insurance   46, 155
  Jointly Owned   120, 152
  Leased   67, 158
  Lost Title   67
  Transfer   152-157
  Value of   155

N

NATIONAL
  Center for
    Health Statistics   217
  Personnel Records   61

NECESSITIES   89, 90

NEGLECTFUL PARENT   137

NET
  Probate Estate   132, 133
  Worth   235

NEXT OF KIN   15, 22, 31, 61
    120, 150, 163, 238

NON-MARITAL CHILD   136

NON-PROBATE TRANSFER
    152, 211, 224

NOTICE TO CREDITORS
    58, 97, 171, 166

NURSING HOME   95, 96

O

OFFICE OF PERSONNEL
    MANAGEMENT   34, 233

ORGAN
  Donor Card   5
  Procurement Organization
    5, 7

OUT OF STATE
  Account   74
  Burial   18
  Deed   72, 125
  Property   81, 125, 169, 202
  Residence   82
  Will   82

OVERWEIGHT, decedent   16

P

PACEMAKER   16

PATERNITY   33, 136

PAY ON DEATH ACCOUNT
    190, 215, 229

PENSION
  Company   35
  Fund   27
  Government   34, 233
  Lost   78
  Plans   57, 104, 244

PERSONAL
  Effects   150, 151
  Property   107, 150, 222

PERSONAL REPRESENTATIVE
  Appoint   29, 174, 219, 220
  Fee   177, 220, 221

PER STIRPES   132, 133, 191

POST OFFICE BOX   63

POUR OVER WILL 212

POWER OF ATTORNEY 237

PRE-NEED SALES CONTRACT 10

PREMARITAL AGREEMENT
        145, 237, 242, 243

PROBATE
  Ancillary Admin. 81, 202
  Avoiding 188
  Cost of 110
  Full Administration 172

PRO BONO 102

PROPERTY
  Abandoned/Unclaimed
        75, 76
  Held in Trust 117, 127,190
        192, 204, 207, 211
  Joint 93, 117-122, 125, 138
        159, 188, 189, 196
  Out of State 81, 125, 169, 202
  Tax 92
  Transfer Of 150, 168, 169

Q
QUALIFIED RETIRE. PLAN 36, 57

R
REAL PROPERTY
  Beneficiary Of 43
  Gift of 192-201
  Held in Trust 117, 128, 204
  Owned Jointly 121-123
        125, 188, 196
  Unclaimed 75, 76
  Transfer of 168, 169

RECORDS
  Business 62, 69
  Court 186
  Financial 66
  Locating 61
  Military 61
  Organizing 232
  Tax 74, 186, 238

REMAINDER INTEREST 124

RESIDENCE, Leased 69

REGISTERED AGENT 50

RESIDUARY BENEF. 154, 222

REVOCABLE LIVING TRUST
        203-214, 245

RIGHT OF SURVIVORSHIP
        93, 117-119, 121, 122
        159, 169, 188, 196, 202, 243

RULES OF DESCENT AND
  DISTRIBUTION
        15, 31, 81, 120, 132-134
        139, 142, 150, 219

S
SAFE DEPOSIT BOX 84, 85
        164, 167, 208, 209, 228
        231, 232, 234, 237

SAME SEX MARRIAGE 131

SECURITIES
  Account 57, 191, 192
  Held Jointly 119
  Transfer on Death 191, 192

SENIOR HEALTH INSURANCE
   PROGRAM   102

SETTLOR   44, 203, 204, 208

SIMULTANEOUS DEATH   138

SMALL ESTATE AFFIDAVIT
          160, 163-167, 188

SNOWMOBILE   68, 161

SOCIAL SECURITY
          27, 32, 33, 78

SPECIFIC GIFT   135, 222, 224

SPENDTHRIFT TRUST   207, 208

SPOUSE
  Award   108, 165
  Debts   89-92
  Exempt Property   107
  Health Insur.   53, 54
  Homestead   42, 109
  IRA   36
  Of Veteran   21
  Pension benefits   34
  Premarital Agreement
       145, 237, 242, 243
  Social Sec. Benefits 32

  SSI   200

STATE AGENCIES,
  Attorney General
    (Crime Victim)   23
  County Assessor   157
  Dept. of Finances &
    Professional Regulation 48
  Dept. of Natural Resources
            68, 76, 159
  Dept. of Prof. Regulation 25
  Dept. of Public Health
           28, 129, 168
  Dept. of Revenue 74, 77, 156
  Dept. of Transportation
              70, 161
  Division of Aeronautics 161
  Division of Vital Records 28
  Driver Services Dept. 156
  Office of State Treasurer 75
  Secretary of State
          50, 67, 78, 120
  Vehicle Services Dept. 120
  Vital Records   27, 28, 61

STATUTE OF LIMITATIONS
             113, 114

STATUTES, FEDERAL
CODE OF FED. REGULATIONS
  40 CFR 229.1   17

FEDERAL TRADE
  COMMISSION RULES
  453.2   11, 12
  453.3   14
  453.4   12
  453.5   12

UNITED STATES CODE (U.S.C.)	
26 U.S.C. 121	42
26 U.S.C. 406	96
26 U.S.C. 1022	41
26 U.S.C. 2503	38
29 U.S.C. 1162	53
29 U.S.C. 1163	53
29 U.S.C. 1165	53
40 USC 274	9
42 U.S.C.1396	103
42 U.S.C 1395I	95

ILLINOIS COMPILED STATUTES ("ILCS")	
35 ILCS 5/201	163
35 ILCS 5/208	43, 198
35 ILCS 5/505	37
35 ILCS 157/10-15	161
35 ILCS 200/15-10	43
35 ILCS 200/15-20	43
35 ILCS 200/15-170	43, 198
35 ILCS 200/15-175	43
35 ILCS 405/2	39
35 ILCS 515/1	68, 157
35 ILCS 515/4	68, 157
55 ILCS 5/5-27001	24
55 ILCS 5/5-27002	24
55 ILCS 5/5-27003	24
205 ILCS 625/3	190
205 ILCS 625/4	190
215 ILCS 5/367.2	54
215 ILCS 5/367.2-5	54
215 ILCS 5/357.31	54
225 ILCS 41/5-5	25
225 ILCS 41/15-75	14, 25
410 ILCS 18/15	15
410 ILCS 18/20	16
410 ILCS 18/25	17
410 ILCS 18/35	16
410 ILCS 505/2	2
410 ILCS 510/1	24
410 ILCS 535/18	3, 27
620 ILCS 5/7	70
620 ILCS 5/42	70
625 ILCS 5/3-101	68
625 ILCS 5/3-114	120, 152
625 ILCS 40/3-1	68, 161
625 ILCS 40/3-11	161
625 ILCS 45/3-1	159
625 ILCS 45/3A-15	159, 160
625 ILCS 45/3C-6	76
625 ILCS 45/3C-8	76
735 ILCS 5/2-1403	205, 207
735 ILCS 5/12-901	108, 198
735 ILCS 5/12-902	108
735 ILCS 5/12-1001	105
735 ILCS 5/12-1003	150
735 ILCS 5/12-1006	104
740 ILCS 45/10.1	23
740 ILCS 45/6.1	23
740 ILCS 45/18	105
740 ILCS 180/2	22, 105, 113
750 ILCS 5/201	129
750 ILCS 5/208	129
750 ILCS 5/212	130
750 ILCS 5/213.1	131
750 ILCS 5/214	130
750 ILCS 5/216	130
750 ILCS 5/217	130
750 ILCS 10/4(a)(3)	145
750 ILCS 10/6	243
750 ILCS 10/7	242
750 ILCS 65/2	90
750 ILCS 65/15	90, 91

STATUTES, ILLINOIS
755 ILCS 5/2-1	132-134, 211
755 ILCS 5/2-2	136, 137
755 ILCS 5/2-3	136
755 ILCS 5/2-4	135
755 ILCS 5/2-5	145
755 ILCS 5/2-6	139
755 ILCS 5/2-6.5	137
755 ILCS 5/2-8	145, 211
755 ILCS 5/3-1	138
755 ILCS 5/4-1	140
755 ILCS 5/4-3	141, 143, 226
755 ILCS 5/4-4	212
755 ILCS 5/4-6	142
755 ILCS 5/4-7	84, 243
755 ILCS 5/4-7(a)	244
755 ILCS 5/4-10	136, 145
755 ILCS 5/5-1	81
755 ILCS 5/6-1	80, 84
755 ILCS 5/6-4	84, 175
755 ILCS 5/6-7	80
755 ILCS 5/6-13	174, 176
755 ILCS 5/6-14	6
755 ILCS 5/7	210, 214
755 ILCS 5/7-1	82
755 ILCS 5/7-4	82
755 ILCS 5/9-3	31, 172
755 ILCS 5/9-5	172, 175
755 ILCS 5/9-8	170, 171
755 ILCS 5/10-1	26
755 ILCS 5/10-4	26
755 ILCS 5/11-5	221
755 ILCS 5/11-5.3	221
755 ILCS 5/11a-2	204, 206
755 ILCS 5/11a-3	204, 206
755 ILCS 5/11a-18	206
755 ILCS 5/12-1	176
755 ILCS 5/12-4	176, 204, 225
755 ILCS 5/14-1	179, 204, 206
755 ILCS 5/14-2	179
755 ILCS 5/15-1	108, 109, 211, 228
755 ILCS 5/15-2	108
755 ILCS 5/16-1	208
755 ILCS 5/16-2	208
755 ILCS 5/18-1.1	106
755 ILCS 5/18-3	97, 113
755 ILCS 5/18-10	110-112
755 ILCS 5/18-12	113
755 ILCS 5/20-1	146
755 ILCS 5/24-1	180, 181
755 ILCS 5/24-11	204, 206
755 ILCS 5/24-16	181
755 ILCS 5/24-18	178
755 ILCS 5/24-19	205, 207
755 ILCS 5/25-1	164-167
755 ILCS 5/25-2	165
755 ILCS 5/27-1	177, 204, 220
755 ILCS 5/27-2	178, 204, 220
755 ILCS 5/28-1	173
755 ILCS 5/28-2	173, 176
755 ILCS 5/28-4	225
755 ILCS 5/28-5	175
755 ILCS 5/28-6	179
755 ILCS 5/28-7	173
755 ILCS 5/28-8	173
755 ILCS 5/28-11	180
755 ILCS 15/1	85-87
755 ILCS 45/2-4(b)	246
755 ILCS 50/5-5	5, 6
755 ILCS 50/15-5	24

STATUTES, ILLINOIS
  760 ILCS 5/3   127
  760 ILCS 5/11   44
  760 ILCS 5/15-1   207, 209
  760 ILCS 15/6(a)   208
  760 ILCS 15/6(f)   208

  760 ILCS 20/4   194
  760 ILCS 20/5   194
  760 ILCS 20/8   193
  760 ILCS 20/10   194
  760 ILCS 20/11   195
  760 ILCS 20/13   195
  760 ILCS 20/15   195
  760 ILCS 20/16   195
  760 ILCS 20/20   195
  760 ILCS 20/21   194
  760 ILCS 35/1(a)   243

  765 ILCS 1005/1   122, 123
  765 ILCS 1005/1c   123, 244
  765 ILCS 1005/2   93, 94
  765 ILCS 1005/2a   118, 189
  765 ILCS 1005/2b   119
  765 ILCS 1005/2c   152
  765 ILCS 1005/2e   120
  765 ILCS 1025/2   75
  765 ILCS 1025/2a   75
  765 ILCS 1025/3   75
  765 ILCS 1025/4   75
  765 ILCS 1025/12   75
  765 ILCS 1025/17   75

  805 ILCS 105/5-10   50
  815 ILCS 10/2   192
  815 ILCS 10/5   191, 192
  815 ILCS 10/6   192
  815 ILCS 10/7   191, 192
  815 ILCS 10/10   191

STATUTORY
  Custodial Claim
      106, 145, 146
  Share   211

STEPPED-UP BASIS
      41, 199, 238

SUCCESSOR TRUSTEE
      44, 127, 203, 204
      206-210, 228

SUMMARY ADMINISTRATION'
      170, 171, 188

SUPERVISED ADMINISTRATION
      173, 175, 176, 225

T

TAX
  Aircraft Use   161
  Capital Gains
      41, 42, 186, 197, 238
  Estate   38-41, 81, 121, 181
      199, 202, 205, 224, 229
  Gift Tax   38, 40, 138
  Income Tax   37, 43, 73
      77, 162, 163, 198
  Property   92, 198
  Records   74, 186, 238
  Stepped-up   41, 199, 238
  Watercraft Use   160

TAXABLE ESTATE   38, 94, 213

TENANTS BY ENTIRETY
      123, 168

TENANTS IN COMMON
      94, 122, 149, 168
      169, 190, 202, 203, 243

TITLE INSURANCE 71, 233, 234

TOTTEN TRUST   127

TRANSFER OF ASSETS
  Aircraft   161
  Bank Account   152
  Income tax refund   77, 162
  Mobile home   157
  Motor vehicle   152-157
  Non-Probate   152, 211, 224
  Personal Property   150, 222
  Real Property   150, 168, 169
  Securities   191, 192, 152, 212
  To Minor   193-195
  Watercraft   159, 160

TRANSFER ON DEATH (TOD)
  Security   191, 192, 152, 212

TRUST
  Bank Account   127, 190, 192
  Beneficiary   44, 117, 204
  Inter Vivos   203
  Property   117, 127,190
        192, 204, 207, 211
  Real Property   117, 128, 204
  Revocable Living
        203-214, 245
  Spendthrift   207, 208

TRUSTEE
        44, 127, 128, 203, 204

U
UNCLAIMED
  Body   24
  Property   75, 76

UNDUE INFLUENCE   142

UNIFORM TRANSFERS
  TO MINORS   193-195

V
VEHICLE SERVICE DEPT   120

VETERANS
  Administration   20-21
  Burial   19-21
  Indigent   24
  National Cemetery   19
  Spouse   21

VICTIM COMPENSATION   23

VITAL RECORDS   27, 28, 61

W
WATERCRAFT   76, 159, 160

WIDOW (see spouse)

WILL
  Challenging   140
  Change Beneficiary   56, 244
  Copy of   84
  File with court   80
  Foreign   82
  Holographic   141
  Missing Will   83
  Pour Over Will   212
  Preparing a Will   226
  Revoke   84, 244
  Storing the Will   226
  Verbal   143

WORKER'S COMP.   22

WRONGFUL DEATH   22, 105

WEB SITES

PAGE	ORGANIZATION	WEB ADDRESS
83	Amer. Assoc. of Retired Persons	http://www.research.aarp.org
48	Amer. Cncl. Life Insurers	http://www.acli.com
70	Federal Aviation Administration	http://www.faa.gov
vii	Federal Statutes	http://www4.law.cornell.edu/uscode
73	IRS	http://www.irs.gov
52	Medicare	http://www.medicare.gov
61	National Archives and Records Administration	http://www.vetrecs.archives.gov
78	Pension Benefit Guar. Corp.	http://wwwpbgc.gov
33	Social Security Admin.	http://www.ssa.gov
54	U.S. Dept. of Labor	http://www.dol.gov/
34	U.S. Office Personal Mgmt	http://www.opm.gov
63	U.S. Post Office	http://www.uspo.com
21	Veteran's Administration	http://www.va.gov
21	Veteran's Admin. Cemetery	http://www.cem.va.gov

ILLINOIS WEB SITES

PAGE ORGANIZATION WEB ADDRESS

159 Dept. of Natural Resources http://www.dnr.state.il.us

37 Dept. of Revenue http://www.revenue.state.il.us

161 Dept. of Transportation http://www.dot.state.il.us

51 Division of Insurance http://www.ins.state.il.us

153 Driver Services Department
 http://www.cyberdriveillinois.com

23 Illinois Attorney General (Crime Victims)
 http://www.ag.state.il.us

43 Illinois Property Taxes http://www.ILtax.com

50 Illinois Secretary of State http://www.sos.state.il.us

xiii Illinois State Bar Association http://www.illinoisbar.org

75 Illinois State Treasurers Office htttp://www.cashdash.net

vii Illinois Statutes http://www.ilga.gov/legislation

28 Vital Records Registry
 http://www.idph.state.il.us/vitalrecords

166 Illinois Statutes are referenced in
Guiding Those Left Behind In Illinois

Each state has its own set of laws relating to the settlement of a person's Estate. The laws that are referenced in this book are very different from the laws of other states.

The author is in now in the process of "translating"
Guiding Those Left Behind
for the rest of the states, that is, writing state specific books that explain how to settle the affairs of someone who dies in the given state.

Books for the following states are now in print:
ALABAMA, ARIZONA, ARKANSAS, CALIFORNIA
CONNECTICUT, FLORIDA, GEORGIA, HAWAII
ILLINOIS, INDIANA, IOWA, KANSAS, KENTUCKY
LOUISIANA, MAINE, MASSACHUSETTS
MARYLAND, MICHIGAN, MINNESOTA, MISSOURI
MISSISSIPPI, NEW JERSEY, NEW YORK
NORTH CAROLINA, OHIO, OKLAHOMA
PENNSYLVANIA, SOUTH CAROLINA, TENNESSEE
TEXAS, VIRGINIA, WASHINGTON, WISCONSIN

Readers of this book can purchase *Guiding Those Left Behind* for $24. This includes shipping and handling.

To order or to check for book availability in other states call Eagle Publishing Company at (800) 824-0823.
- or -
Visit our Web site http://www.eaglepublishing.com

BOOK REVIEWS OF *Guiding Those Left Behind*

ARIZONA
Ben T. Traywick of the Tombstone Epitaph said "This book is an excellent reference book that simplifies all the necessary tasks that must be done when there is a death in the family. There is even an explanation as to how you can arrange your own estate so that your heirs will not be left with a multitude of nagging problems." "The reviewer has been going through probate for two years with no end yet in sight. This book at the beginning two year ago would have helped immensely."

CALIFORNIA
Margot Petit Nichols of the Carmel Pine Cone called it a ". . .TRULY RIVETING READ." " . . . I could scarcely put it down." "This is a book that we should all have, either on our book shelves or thoughtfully placed with our important papers."

OTHER BOOKS BY AMELIA E. POHL

Beyond Grief To Acceptance and Peace

AMELIA E. POHL and the noted psychologist BARBARA J. SIMMONDS, Ph.d, have written a book for those families who have suffered a loss.

- ✧ What to say to the bereaved
- ✧ How to help a child through the loss
- ✧ Strategies to adjust to a new life-style
- ✧ When and where to seek assistance.

80 pages   6" X 9" $10 includes Shipping and Handling
TO ORDER CALL (800) 824-0823.

A Will is Not Enough...

Many people who have a Will think that they have their affairs in order. They believe that their Will can take care of any problem that may arise. But the primary function of a Will is to distribute property to people named in a Will. A Will cannot:

- ⇨ Protect your assets and limit your debt
- ⇨ Provide care for a minor or disabled child
- ⇨ Avoid Guardianship
- ⇨ Appoint someone to make your health care decisions should you be unable to do so
- ⇨ Appoint someone to handle your finances should you be unable to do so
- ⇨ Arrange to pay for your health care should you need long term nursing care, including qualifying for MEDICAID.

AMELIA E. POHL, Esq. has written a series of state specific books explaining how to do all of these things. This new book series is a continuation of this book. It builds on basic Estate Planning concepts introduced in Chapter 7 of this book and then goes on to introduce other, more sophisticated, Estate Planning methods. Although the topics are sophisticated, the writing style is the same as in this book. It is written in plain English. It is intended for use by the average person.

A Will Is Not Enough is now available for:
ARIZONA, CALIFORNIA, CONNECTICUT, COLORADO
FLORIDA, GEORGIA, HAWAII, INDIANA, ILLINOIS, MARYLAND
MICHIGAN, MASSACHUSETTS, NEBRASKA, NEW JERSEY
NEW MEXICO, NEW YORK, OREGON, PENNSYLVANIA
TEXAS, VIRGINIA, WASHINGTON, WISCONSIN.

Readers of this book can purchase *A Will Is Not Enough* for $25. This includes shipping and handling. To check for book availability in other states call Eagle Publishing Company

How To Defend Yourself Against Your Lawyer

is a book about the unhappy experiences people have with their lawyers, beginning with that of the author AMELIA E. POHL. She became involved in a law suit and found herself in the role of client, rather than lawyer. She become concerned about lawyers who do not provide their clients with loyalty and respect. This book is a result of those concerns.

The book is divided into chapters that cover the most common problems that take people to a lawyer: divorce, probate, criminal, personal injury, starting a business, making a Will, buying a house, etc. Each chapter tells of the misadventures of the unwary as they sought the services of a lawyer without a clue as to what they were "buying." This book is funny, sad, interesting, but most of all informative. It tells the reader how to become a savvy consumer, i.e., how to find the right lawyer for the right job. If you ever find the need to employ a lawyer, you will be glad you read this book.

Copyright 2004   272 pages 6" X 9"   soft cover
$20 includes Shipping and Handling

BOOK REVIEW

TED KREITER of the SATURDAY EVENING POST said "Horror fans, forget about those tawdry tales of ghosts and vampires. Pick up Amelia E. Pohl's *How To Defend Yourself Against Your Lawyer* to read some really scary stuff. Like the story . . . of the grieving widow, Ethel, whose husband died shortly after a lawyer drafted a sweetheart will for the two of them. . . . Six months in attorney's fees later, Ethel learned that she already had her husband's money because it never needed to go through probate! . . Ethel then went out and found a good lawyer for $1,000 who was able to get her $5,000 back. You do the math. . . Following Pohl's useful advice could save a person much more than money."

It is the goal of EAGLE PUBLISHING COMPANY to keep our publications fresh.

As we receive information about changes to the federal or state law we will post an update to this edition at our Web site.

http://www.eaglepublishing.com